# WALK
## OF THE
# WEEK

# WALK OF THE WEEK

**Peter Evans**

&

James McDonald

Illustrated by

**Glen McBeth**

MERCAT PRESS
EDINBURGH
www.mercatpress.com

First published in 2004 by
**Mercat Press Ltd.**
**10 Coates Crescent**
**Edinburgh EH3 7AL**
**www.mercatpress.com**

Design
**Angus Bremner, www.bremnerdesign.co.uk**

Cover design
**Angus Bremner/Catherine Read**

ISBN: 184183 0747

Printed in Spain by
**Graficas Santamaria**

The walks originally appeared in *Scotland on Sunday* and are reproduced by
permission of Scotsman Publications Ltd.

# CONTENTS

Introduction

Locations

The walks

1 The Deil's Cauldron
2 Ballater Bridges
3 St Abb's Head
4 Glen Finglas
5 Ben Lomond
6 Roslin Glen
7 Mount Keen
8 The Ochils
9 Monument Hill, Dalmally
10 The Knock of Crieff
11 The Cobbler
12 The Greenock Cut
13 St Andrews
14 Railway Ramble, Killin
15 The Whangie
16 Ben Venue
17 Anstruther to Crail
18 Ben A'an
19 Fetlar (Shetland)
20 Ben Vrackie
21 Stacks of Duncansby
22 Meikle Bin
23 Ben Nevis
24 Callendar Park
25 The Eildon Hills
26 Falls of Clyde
27 Linlithgow to Cockleroy

28 Tinto Hill
29 Schiehallion
30 Beinn Eighe
31 Birnam Hill
32 Dun Caan
33 Loch an Eilein
34 Loch Trool
35 Largo Law
36 North Berwick Law
37 Castle to Calton Hill
38 Falkland & East Lomond
39 Callander Crags
40 The Burns Trail
41 The Pap of Glencoe
42 West Lomond
43 Arthur's Seat
44 Buachaille Etive Beag
45 Dumgoyne
46 Duns Law & Hen Poo
47 Beinn Resipol
48 Braemar Circuit
49 Isle of Kerrera
50 Loch Etive Shore
51 Elie to Shell Bay
52 Dun da Lamh

Biographies

Walks rating Index

Alphabetical index

# INTRODUCTION

FROM the top of Ben Nevis in the rugged west, to the gentler seascape of the Fife coast in the east, and from the vast open emptiness of the far north to the rolling hills of the Borders, Scotland's scenic variety is truly amazing. Covering a huge land mass – often underestimated by those not familiar with it – the country has only 10 per cent of Britain's population, mostly concentrated in the central belt, marked on either side by the great cities of Glasgow and Edinburgh, the capital. There is ample opportunity, then, for the walker seeking solitude, to find it in abundance in the Scottish countryside. It is possible to do some of the remoter walks in this book and not see a soul all day. With a traditional freedom of access comes the responsibility to treat the countryside with respect. Anyone following these walks is urged strongly to do so – for the benefit of wildlife and the environment and also to ensure that future generations can continue to enjoy the wonderful legacy that nature has bestowed. The red stag stalking season takes place from July 1 to Oct 20. Recorded phone messages on some estates allow walkers to avoid sensitive areas. Further information is available on *www.hillphones.info*.

Quite apart from the obvious attractions of scenery and wildlife, Scotland also has much more to offer the inquisitive walker. History figures large in the Scottish landscape, with influences from early Celtic tribes to the Romans and later, to territorial clashes between the Scots and the English and scenes of bloody conflict. It's all there for those who wish to seek it out, pause and explore a while the sites of interest referred to in this book.

If there is one thing certain about the weather in Scotland, it is uncertainty. There are gloriously sunny days, very wet and very cold ones. It is prudent to go equipped for changing conditions, particularly on higher level outings into the mountains, and to listen carefully to weather forecasts before setting out. While walks descriptions are as accurate as they can be, changes on the ground may be encountered through land management activities and forestry operations. In the main, however, there should be few problems providing you exercise common sense. The directions offer a good general guide, but the relevant Ordnance Survey or other maps should be carried, together with a compass and the ability to use it, especially in wilder terrain.

One lifetime is scarcely enough to explore all that Scotland's great outdoors temptingly lays before those who don a pair of walking boots and head into the countryside. From that standpoint any guidebook is inadequate. What we have tried to do in this one is bring together a collection of walks regarded by the authors

as some of the best they have enjoyed. The routes range from easy strolls to much more demanding treks up Munros – peaks over 3,000ft. In winter they will often demand mountaineering skills, with the need to carry an ice-axe and crampons, but in summer should not be beyond the capability of any reasonably fit walker. All the routes have been selected from a series published over several years in *Scotland on Sunday*. With positive feedback coming both from readers of the paper and countryside agencies, it was felt appropriate to bring a collection together in a convenient and colourful compilation, offering a walk for every week of the year.

Since the Walk of the Week series began there have been a variety of authors, with Peter Evans the present incumbent. The walks that appear in this volume were written by him and his immediate predecessor, James McDonald. We hope you gain as much enjoyment from them as we have.

**Peter Evans**

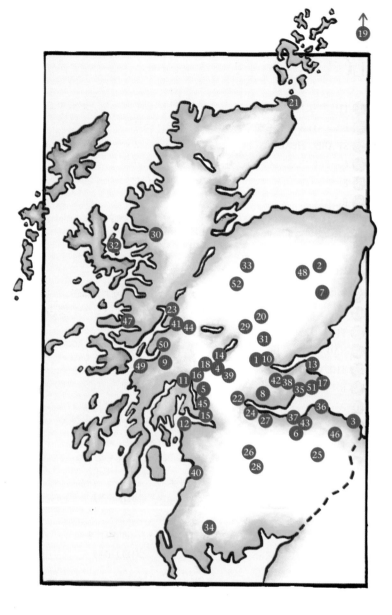

# LOCATIONS

1. THE DEIL'S CAULDRON
2. BALLATER BRIDGES
3. ST ABB'S HEAD
4. GLEN FINGLAS
5. BEN LOMOND
6. ROSLIN GLEN
7. MOUNT KEEN
8. THE OCHILS
9. MONUMENT HILL
10. THE KNOCK OF CRIEFF
11. THE COBBLER
12. THE GREENOCK CUT
13. ST ANDREWS
14. RAILWAY RAMBLE, KILLIN
15. THE WHANGIE
16. BEN VENUE
17. ANSTRUTHER TO CRAIL
18. BEN A'AN
19. FETLAR (SHETLAND)
20. BEN VRACKIE
21. STACKS OF DUNCANSBY
22. MEIKLE BIN
23. BEN NEVIS
24. CALLENDAR PARK
25. THE EILDON HILLS
26. FALLS OF CLYDE
27. LINLITHGOW TO COCKLEROY
28. TINTO HILL
29. SCHIEHALLION
30. BEINN EIGHE
31. BIRNAM HILL
32. DUN CAAN
33. LOCH AN EILEIN
34. LOCH TROOL
35. LARGO LAW
36. NORTH BERWICK LAW
37. CASTLE TO CALTON HILL
38. FALKLAND & EAST LOMOND
39. CALLANDER CRAGS
40. THE BURNS TRAIL
41. THE PAP OF GLENCOE
42. WEST LOMOND
43. ARTHUR'S SEAT
44. BUACHAILLE ETIVE BEAG
45. DUMGOYNE
46. DUNS LAW & HEN POO
47. BEINN RESIPOL
48. BRAEMAR CIRCUIT
49. ISLE OF KERRERA
50. LOCH ETIVE SHORE
51. ELIE TO SHELL BAY
52. DUN DA LAMH

# THE DEIL'S CAULDRON

Waterfalls are always an attractive feature for walkers and this one, when the River Lednock is in spate, can be quite spectacular, cascading into a boiling pool with the inevitable supernatural legend attached.

**THEME** Goblins and fairies in one guise or another are no strangers to the Scottish countryside, with stories abounding as to their deeds, both good and evil. In this case we have a rather nasty water elf called Uris-chidh in Gaelic, who enticed victims into the foaming cauldron of water at the base of a waterfall. A viewing platform provides a good view. Comrie, where the walk starts, has acquired a reputation as 'the shaky town' because of the number of earthquakes recorded there – more than anywhere else in Britain. The first to be monitored was in 1788, and early equipment used for measuring quakes is on display at Earthquake House, just west of the town. The phenomenon is thought to be connected to Comrie's position on the Highland boundary fault. On Dunmore Hill, which can be visited on the walk and is an impressive viewpoint, is a monument to Henry Dundas, a powerful parliamentarian holding numerous offices of state, who was designated Viscount Melville. Comrie has a history of settlement by the Romans, who called it Victoria, then later the Picts, who dubbed it Aberlednock.

**ROUTE** From the car park in School Road, Comrie, turn right and walk along the main street. Where the road bears sharply left go straight on, following a Glen Lednock walk sign. Turn right and continue along the track through woodland. The route arrives at the banks of the Lednock. Continue uphill, climbing high above the river. Where the path levels beside a minor road, go right and straight on beside a wall to reach wooden steps leading down to the viewing platform for the Deil's Cauldron. Return to the top and walk along the minor road, making a detour up to Melville Monument if desired. After less than half a mile a sign is reached pointing the way along a rough track. Cross a wooden bridge over the Lednock. Turn right and after crossing a stile walk along a farm track. Then, bearing very gradually left, head towards forestry. Go through a gate into the trees and along the track. At a 'Circular Walk' sign continue straight on and at a junction of tracks and another waymarker, turn right. Follow the path which descends quite steeply back down to rejoin the Lednock and into the town.

| MAP | OS 52 Pitlochry to Crieff |
|---|---|
| DISTANCE | 4.5 miles (7km) |
| RATING | Easy. Paths, tracks and minor road |
| GEAR | Boots and a waterproof |

# BALLATER BRIDGES

Closely associated with the Royal Family, Ballater developed as a spa town in Queen Victoria's time. The health-giving properties of its surrounding countryside certainly have much to offer walkers.

**THEMES** The proximity of Balmoral Castle, the royals' Highland hame, and of Crathie Kirk, where they worship when in residence, have assured Ballater a place on the tourist map. Wandering along its streets, it's possible to spot the shops that have been given the regal seal of approval to supply goods to the family. Prince Charles in particular has long been fond of the area, using it as the setting for his Old Man of Lochnagar story and for paintings. In winter raiment, the cliffs of Lochnagar, with the loch sitting in a bowl beneath them, are an unforgettable sight. Small wonder, then, that they have such a powerful attraction for an outdoor-loving prince and thousands of walkers. It was through an event in 1760 when an elderly woman drank from a spring at Pannanich, near Ballater, and was cured of scrofula – a form of tuberculosis – that the town's reputation as a spa was acquired. The last bridge crossed on our walk, Postie's Leap, got its name after a postman jumped to his death in the ravine below. The poor chap had been jilted on the eve of his wedding.

**ROUTE** Leaving Station Square in Ballater, turn left to reach the Royal Bridge, spanning the River Dee. It was opened by Queen Victoria in 1885. Go over the bridge and turn right. Follow the B976 to cross two more bridges. The road bears hard right over yet another bridge with Glenmuick churchyard just after it on the left. John Mitchell was buried here in 1722 having reached the remarkable age of 126. Further along the road, look out for a track on the right, just past a short wooded stretch. Follow the track for some distance through dense conifer woods to reach shapely Polhollick Bridge, crossing the Dee again. After the distinctive white metal bridge the track continues to the A93. Turn right along the road for a short distance and cross very carefully to mount some steps giving access to a path, heading back towards Ballater. Cross the A 939 coming down from the left and walk on to where the path rejoins the A93 at Bridge of Gairn. Cross the bridge and look for an opening on the right that gives access to a path leading down to what should have been, in the 19th century, the Braemar to Ballater railway line. It was never built, but provides a pleasant walking surface for the final stretch of the walk back to Ballater.

| | |
|---|---|
| **MAP** | OS 37 Ballater |
| **DISTANCE** | 5.5 miles (9km) |
| **RATING** | Easy. Paths, tracks and roads |
| **GEAR** | Boots and waterproofs |

# ST ABB'S HEAD

Seabirds and religion are the dominant features of this walk along a section of Scotland's most captivatingly beautiful coastline.

**THEMES** North of St Abbs is Dunbar, famous as the birthplace of John Muir, Scotland's best known conservationist and father of the national parks concept through Yosemite in America. A country park has been created at Dunbar in Muir's memory. His vision has at last come home to his native land with the designation of the first national park north of the Border, covering Loch Lomond and the Trossachs. St Abb's Head is a national nature reserve, jointly managed by the National Trust for Scotland and the Scottish Wildlife Trust. In spring and early summer thousands of seabirds throng the cliffs - a sight not easily forgotten. This rugged coastline is one of their most important sites for nesting and breeding in Britain. At Cockburnspath, between Dunbar and St Abbs, is the terminal point for one of Scotland's long distance footpaths, the Southern Upland Way. Less well known than its much more popular cousin the West Highland Way further north, it is a challenging route for walkers. At Coldingham village is a 900-year-old priory established by Edgar, king of the Scots. It was largely rebuilt in the 17th century and still serves as the parish church.

**ROUTE** From the visitor centre at Northfield, which is worth looking round before you start, head north along the road towards St Abb's Head. The road makes an abrupt right turn at Pettico Wick, where there is a striking view along the coastline. Continue to the lighthouse and the cliffs at St Abb's Head. Pick up the cliff path heading south behind Kirk Hill, where colourful thrift carpets the ground in summer. Go over a stile and follow the path onwards, rejoining the coast again at Horsecastle Bay. Continue over Bell Hill, with a panoramic view of St Abbs village and beyond. Carry on past a small wooded area to a road and turn left, making for the attractive haven of St Abbs harbour. A path climbs out of the harbour. Turn left at the top. Walk between houses and follow the path right to reach sandy Coldingham Bay. Take the road leading out of the bay towards Coldingham itself. Visit the priory then backtrack along the B6438 that leads to St Abbs. In about half a mile break off right along the old Creel Road, eventually arriving back at St Abbs village. Turn left on entering the village, then left again for Northfield.

St Abb's Head

Visitor's
Centre

St Abbs

Coldingham

| MAP | OS 67 Duns, Dunbar and Eyemouth area |
|---|---|
| DISTANCE | 6 miles (10km) |
| RATING | Moderate. Firm paths, sand and rocky shoreline |
| GEAR | Boots and waterproofs |

# GLEN FINGLAS

Autumn is a good time of year to do this walk for the magnificent woodland colours prevalent then, but don't disappear in the bog of the horse!

**THEMES** Although a long walk, this does not involve much ascent, is easy to follow and on firm surfaces all the way. Autumn is an excellent time to enjoy it, as the trees and bracken don their multi-coloured seasonal overcoat. Glen Finglas once formed part of a royal hunting forest. Novelist Sir Walter Scott, inextricably linked to the Trossachs, mentioned Finglas Water in *The Lady of the Lake* and wrote at greater length about the area in his epic poem *Glenfinlas*. The estate was acquired by the Woodland Trust four years ago. Now the Trust is engaged in a long-term woodland restoration plan spanning 30 to 40 years. Its aim is to restore the native tree cover which once made this place even more beautiful than it is today. Trees such as birch, alder and rowan are being encouraged to propagate naturally as much as possible by cutting out animal overgrazing. The trust has also undertaken the planting of thousands more young saplings grown from seed gathered in the area. Alongside the highest point on the track circling Meall Cala is the Moine nan Each, or bog of the horse. The story goes that a pony boy was bringing a dead stag off the hill, slung over the horse's back. As the pony was led through the bog it sank under the weight and was

lost, unable to escape the cloying peat. Hence the bog acquired its name.

**ROUTE** Brig o' Turk lies off the A821 Callander to Aberfoyle road, winding through the Trossachs. From the village hall, where you are asked to park, walk along the tarmac road ahead in the direction of Glen Finglas reservoir. The road eventually divides, with the right hand fork leading to Glen Finglas. Go through a gate and continue uphill. It's a bit of a trudge, but persevere. The road levels off as the reservoir and its dam come into view below, on the left. Carry on, parallel to the reservoir, following the road down to where it crosses the Casaig burn. Repair work is going on here to restore the road and the culvert underneath. A severe storm washed the road away in 1998 as boulders and water crashed down the burn. The road becomes a track and continues, with fine views, towards the end of the reservoir. At a junction, take the signposted route to Balquhidder, an ancient right of way and drove road. Now it's simply a matter of following the track circling the hill in front of you, Meall Cala. The track winds around to the western side of the hill and finally drops quite steeply down by the Finglas Water to reach the reservoir again.

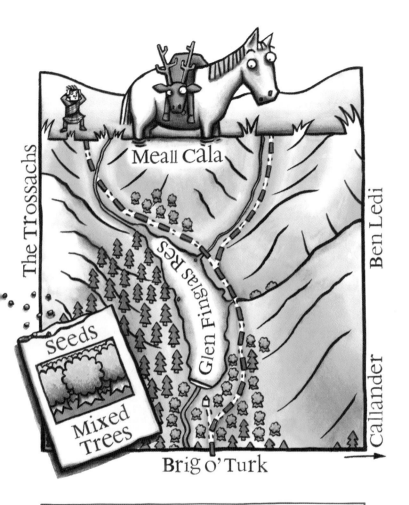

The Trossachs

Meall Cala

Glen Finglas RES

Ben Ledi

Callander

seeds

Mixed Trees

Brig o' Turk

| | |
|---|---|
| **MAP** | OS 57 Stirling and Trossachs |
| **DISTANCE** | 13 miles (21km) |
| **RATING** | Strenuous. Road and track |
| **GEAR** | In autumn and winter, take full hill-walking kit |

# BEN LOMOND

At the time of year when the four-wheel drive really comes into its own, when St Bernards are ready to do their stuff, and when brass monkeys are going about with fear etched on their faces, why do hill-walkers go on to the hills?

**THEMES** A question often asked from the depths of the fireside armchair is why do people go out onto the hills in winter. It's one that's difficult to reconcile when you hear of mountain rescue teams being called out by ill-equipped inadequates summoning assistance on a mobile phone. But when walkers have invested the time and energy learning old-fashioned hill sense, they gain a love of all that is beautiful in nature and a release that no other sport can provide. Dangerous situations can be recognised, assessed and avoided. Armchair critics will never understand the philosophy of true hill-walkers: gangrels who delight in the struggle, summer or winter, who enjoy the contented fatigue after a day on the hills – a feeling that is the essence of their wellbeing. Ben Lomond's commanding position allowed tribes of centuries gone by to spot marauding Vikings approaching their territory. The Scandinavian invaders sailed up neighbouring Loch Long and hauled their longships from the landing place at Arrochar over the pass to Tarbet. From there it was into the boats again to sail down Loch Lomond for a spot of raping and pillaging!

**ROUTE** On crisp, clear winter's day, one of the most popular hills – because of its splendid panoramic views and proximity to the greater populace – is Scotland's most southerly Munro. An early start is recommended, with as much care being taken on the roads getting there as on the hillside itself. From Glasgow, take the A81 and A809 to Drymen, the B837 to Balmaha and the minor road on to Rowardennan, parking at the pier. The path, signed for Ben Lomond, starts behind the public toilets. Ascend through trees for about three quarters of a mile before a gate is reached at the top of the forest. Follow the broad ridge north to where the views of the mountains across Loch Katrine suddenly burst into sight and the path turns west, zig-zagging on to the summit ridge. The summit is reached after negotiating a few bumps. Return the same way.

Ben Lomond

West Highland Way

Loch Lomond

Rowardennan

| | |
|---|---|
| **MAP** | OS Sheet 56, Loch Lomond and Inveraray |
| **DISTANCE** | 7.5 miles (12km) |
| **RATING** | Strenuous. Long mountain path |
| **GEAR** | Full hill-walking kit |

# ROSLIN GLEN

The St Clairs of Roslin have been close to royalty ever since William 'the Seemly', son of William the Conqueror's cousin Waldernus, obtained part of the Barony of Rosslyn from Malcolm Canmore.

**THEMES** William the Seemly's grandson, Henry St Clair, was sent by King William the Lion to the English court to reclaim the disputed territory of Northumberland from King Henry II. Several generations later, another Henry St Clair fought beside Bruce at Bannockburn. With Bruce's death in 1329, Henry's son, Sir William, was one of the Knights Templar to carry the king's heart on the journey to the Holy Land. During a fierce battle with the Moors in Spain, Sir William was killed. Impressed with the courage shown by the Scottish knight, the Moors allowed survivors to take Sir William, and Bruce's heart, back home to Scotland for burial. The heart lies in a casket buried at Melrose Abbey. Rosslyn Chapel, founded in 1446, is remarkable for its carvings representing secular and religious themes. For lovers of the countryside, there are more than 100 images of the Green Man, the pagan figure strangely symbolising great good and great evil. But by far the most intricate carving is the Apprentice Pillar with its legendary link to murder. The pillar was supposedly carved by an apprentice mason

while his master was away in Rome. On his return, so jealous was the master of the apprentice's skill at completing the pillar that he killed him.

**ROUTE** Exit the A720 Edinburgh city bypass at Straiton junction and drive south on the A701 towards Penicuik. At the mining village of Bilston take the B7006 to Roslin, parking at the chapel car park. The walk starts from Old Rosslyn Inn, where a commemorative plaque lists Burns, Sir Walter Scott and the Wordworths among its distinguished visitors. Continue past the graveyard and follow a line of mature oak trees above the glen. This circular walk then takes you left, downhill on to Jacob's Ladder – a long set of steps – past the sewage treatment works, where another left turn takes you into Roslin Glen. Cross the River North Esk by the iron footbridge and stroll along to Rosslyn Castle. Burnt by the English army of Henry the VIII in 1544, it was again besieged and taken by the English in 1650 under the command of General Monk. Now the fortress lies in ruins. From the castle, your final left turn of the day takes you steeply uphill to the graveyard and car park.

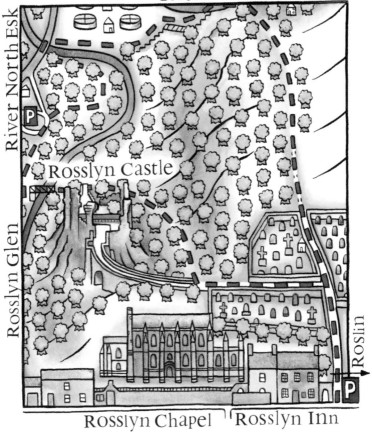

B**7003**

River North Esk

Rosslyn Glen

Rosslyn Castle

Roslin

Rosslyn Chapel   Rosslyn Inn

| | |
|---|---|
| MAP | OS Sheet 66, Edinburgh, Penicuik & North Berwick |
| DISTANCE | 2 miles (3km) |
| RATING | Easy. Landscaped paths and steep stairway |
| GEAR | No special requirements |

# MOUNT KEEN

Scotland's most easterly Munro is a solitary hill providing a fine walk in the rolling countryside of Angus, and offers less resistance than some of the rockier giants in the west.

**THEMES** Mount Keen was my elder daughter's first Munro. She did it the easy way, carried on my back as a baby in a child carrier designed specially for the purpose. Despite a squally shower and a chill wind on the summit, Juliet was chuckling happily, tucked snugly in a waterproof. Be sure to keep very young children warm – they're not moving and you are – and there's no reason why being a parent should stop you getting out in the fresh air. This route up Mount Keen provides an interesting landmark in the form of the Queen's Well – a natural spring from which Queen Victoria reputedly took refreshment in 1861 during one of her many outings in the area. The Angus glens of Esk, Clova, Prosen and Isla are in complete contrast to the rugged territory of Lochaber, Glencoe or Torridon, but no less beautiful in their own right. The countryside is characterised by moorland and gentler hills, seamed by a network of inviting paths and rights of way used by travellers for centuries.

**ROUTE** Start from the car park about three miles west of the little hamlet of Tarfside in Glen Esk. It's at the dividing point between Glen Mark and Glen Lee. If you have time, go and see nearby Loch Lee – a reservoir supplying water to Angus and Kincardineshire. Leaving the car park head straight up Glen Mark. The going is quite easy on a good surface with the Water of Mark for company. Queen's Well is reached in around two miles. Ignore a path to the left following the Water of Mark and continue straight on for Mount Keen. The path now steepens markedly up beside the Ladder Burn on the ancient Mounth road right of way. A succession of zig-zags climbs the southern shoulder of the mountain. Further on the path divides, the Mounth road going to the left, while the right branch leads directly to the summit of Mount Keen. Just before the summit there is a boundary stone with the letter 'B' carved on it. Return by the same route.

Mount Keen

Glen Mark

Queen's Well

Glen Esk

Loch Lee

| | |
|---|---|
| **MAP** | OS 44 Ballater |
| **DISTANCE** | 9 miles there and back (14km) |
| **RATING** | Strenuous. Track and well defined mountain path |
| **GEAR** | Full hill-walking kit |

# THE OCHILS

Their dramatic escarpment, rising steeply above the towns at its foot – once famed for their woollen manufacture – makes these hills highly distinctive.

**THEMES** Dollar Glen, at the start of this walk, is in the care of the National Trust for Scotland. Its plants, birdlife and geological features make it a site of special scientific interest. Dominating the glen is Castle Campbell, a former stronghold of the earls of Argyll. Protestant firebrand John Knox is thought to have stayed at the castle in 1556 and preached a sermon from a rocky knoll, known as John Knox's Pulpit. In reality the message was more likely to have been delivered within the castle walls.

Split by rocky gorges with rushing burns that powered the woollen mills of the past, the area has a history of witchcraft. Margaret Duchil, from Alloa, was tried as a witch in 1658. She confessed to being in league with the devil. Witchcraft was a criminal offence in Scotland until 1763, and between 1590 and 1700 over 4,000 people were executed. Witches were supposed to gather on Gloom Hill above Dollar, and at its foot stands the Wizard's Stone, reputed to mark the spot where a warlock was burnt to death.

**ROUTE** From Dollar, take the path to the left of the local museum that winds up through the glen to arrive at the entrance to Castle Campbell. Looked after by Historic Scotland, it is open to visitors. Now follow the path that leads to the top of Bank Hill, with open views over Dollar and out to the River Forth and Fife in the east. Continue on along the well defined path, climbing steadily to the crest of King's Seat hill. Walk north and descend the hill, veering west to Maddy Moss, then climbing again to gain the top of Andrew Gannel Hill. Take the path westwards towards Ben Cleuch – highest point in the Ochils – which has a direction indicator on its summit. It's possible to make this walk circular by dropping down over an outlying hill, The Law, into Tillicoultry, returning to Dollar by the old railway track known as the Devon Way. From Ben Cleuch descend to a bealach and go over Ben Ever, heading south off it to reach a track skirting The Nebit. This can be followed into Alva. Alternatively, turn west along a grassy path that leads into the lower part of Alva Glen.

Castle Campbell

| | |
|---|---|
| **MAP** | OS 58 Perth to Alloa |
| **DISTANCE** | 7 miles (11km) |
| **RATING** | Moderate. Hill paths |
| **GEAR** | Full hill-walking kit |

Ben Ever

Ben Cleuch

King's Seat Hill

The Law

Gloom Hill

Alva

A91

Dollar

Tillicoultry

# MONUMENT HILL: DALMALLY

Where sheep once caused homes to be abandoned and spread the braes with ruin, now stands a hilltop monument to the local bard, Duncan Ban MacIntyre.

**THEMES** The great Gaelic Bard, Duncan Ban MacIntyre (1724-1812) who fought under the Hanoverian flag at the Battle of Falkirk in 1746, has often been likened to his contemporaries, Burns and Scott. Writing only in Gaelic, having no education in English, MacIntyre's verse *In Praise of Ben Dorian* is said to be as descriptive as Scott's *Lady of the Lake* and the address to Mary Bhan (Fair Haired Mary), his wife, is thought by many to be the best love song ever written in the Celtic tongue. A gamekeeper in Breadalbane and Rannoch after the 1745 rebellion, MacIntyre hated the influx of sheep and the resulting clearances with a passion. As he states in his *Song of Foxes*: "My blessings with the foxes dwell, For that they hunt the sheep so well, For stags will flee and mothers will weep, When gentlemen live to make money by sheep!"

**ROUTE** Take the A82 trunk road north to Tyndrum, then continue on the A85 Oban road to Dalmally, parking in the station car park. Dalmally is superbly situated in the Strath of Orchy, near Loch Awe, and can be used as a base for many walking expeditions in the area. From the station car park, turn left uphill and follow the signs for Monument Hill and Duncan Ban's monument. Cross over a railway bridge and follow the rising track for about one and a half miles. Although the route is tree-lined most of the way, there are sufficient glimpses for you to see the countryside unfold. As you reach the tree line, a short pull up grassy slopes takes you to the MacIntyre monument.

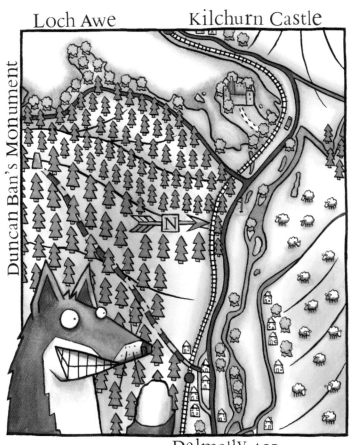

Loch Awe

Kilchurn Castle

Duncan Ban's Monument

N

Dalmally A85

| | |
|---|---|
| **MAP** | Sheet 50, Glen Orchy |
| **DISTANCE** | 4 miles (6km) |
| **RATING** | Easy. A tree-lined, tarmac track |
| **GEAR** | Warm clothing and strong footwear |

# THE KNOCK OF CRIEFF

Once known as the Montpellier of Scotland, Crieff has long been a magnet for tourists. But when the citizens of Crieff rolled out the barrel, not everyone found it a bundle of fun.

**THEMES** Day trippers to Crieff are spoilt for choice for walks in and around the town: Lady Mary's Walk along the banks of the River Earn or the Highland Dyke walk, following the Highland fault line at nearby Muthill and Drummond Castle Gardens, which featured in the film *Rob Roy*. But the jewel in the crown is The Knock. This is a marvellous woodland ramble among deciduous and coniferous trees, offering spectacular views.

**ROUTE** The Knock of Crieff is the prominent wooded hill which stands to the north of the town and is where the area's witches were tried. Tradition says it was here that the Perthshire witch, Kate MacNieven, was placed in a barrel of spikes and rolled over the Craigs that still bear her name. To get there, take the A9 north from Stirling, leaving the dual carriageway at Greenloaning by the A822, arriving at Crieff after passing through Braco and Muthill. Starting your walk from James Square in the centre of town, proceed up Hill Street and Ferntower Road into Knock Road (signposted), where a gate at the top allows access on to the hill after passing through a horse paddock. From here, an obvious path leads to the twin summit, with a viewfinder marking the lower peak and a cairn of stones, marking the true summit, in the middle of a tree enclosure, 450 yards to the north-east. There are many paths criss-crossing The Knock, the most popular being the forestry track circumnavigating the hill.

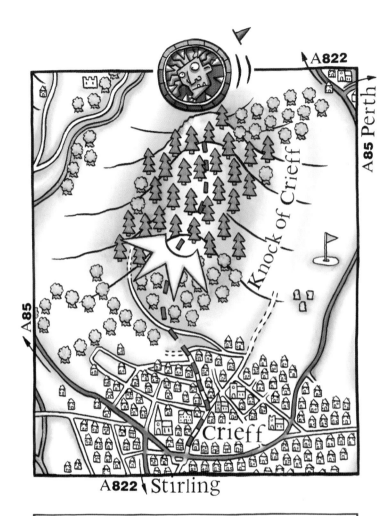

| MAP | OS Sheet 52, Pitlochry to Crieff or 58, Perth to Alloa |
| --- | --- |
| DISTANCE | 5 miles (8km) |
| RATING | Easy. Mostly forest track |
| GEAR | Boots and a waterproof |

# THE COBBLER

Dominating the village of Arrochar, the craggy, serrated profile of Ben Arthur, to give the hill its Sunday-best name, has been a magnet for generations of walkers and climbers.

**THEMES** A combination of three separate tops, The Cobbler's name dates back hundreds of years, deriving from the fanciful picture of a cobbler (the north peak) leaning over his last (the central peak) while his wife Jean (the south peak) looks on. Viewed from the right angle, the central peak – also the true summit – does resemble an upturned boot or cobbler's last. During the depression years of the 1930s The Cobbler became a wild refuge for the hillgoing pioneers who escaped the drab city streets of Glasgow for the countryside. They slept under boulders, walked and climbed, and forged lasting friendships. Alastair Borthwick's classic book *Always a Little Further* recounts many of their adventures. Attaining the actual summit of the hill takes a little nerve. After crawling through a hole, 'threading the needle', a shimmy along an exposed ledge follows. A short scramble emerges on the top for a whoop of triumph. Then resolve must be gathered for the descent, with an intimidating drop facing you before the ledge is traversed to the hole once again. For those whose nerves just won't stand the strain, a friendly climber can usually be prevailed upon to provide the comforting security of a rope.

**ROUTE** There is a spacious car park on the western shore of Loch Long after you pass through Arrochar village and round the head of the loch. Cross the road and head along the path, initially through woodland, which follows the line of an old tramway used in the process of mining a waterway in the hill above. After a while a forestry road is reached. Turn left, along a new route which takes the sting out of the former relentless climb that continued straight up. Wind around to a small reservoir on the left and continue straight on, keeping company with the Allt a' Bhalachain – the Buttermilk Burn. Take a breather at the giant Narnain Boulder before continuing up. The path is now greatly improved from here on over what was formerly a boggy stretch, and makes for a much more pleasant ascent. Aim for the gap between the north peak (on your right) and centre peak and finally turn right over a rocky slab to gain the north peak's top. Reverse the slab and walk along to the centre peak. The south peak is the domain only of climbers. Descend the path to its right and walk along the ridge ahead. Finally descend left to cross the **Buttermilk Burn** again and regain the upward route below the Narnain Boulder.

| | |
|---|---|
| **MAP** | OS 56 Loch Lomond |
| **DISTANCE** | 5.5 miles (9km) |
| **RATING** | Strenuous. Mountain paths, easy rock climb at top |
| **GEAR** | Full hill-walking kit |

# GREENOCK CUT

Water, Water everywhere, nor any drop to drink – that is until Robert Thom came along and engineered the Greenock Cut.

**THEMES** In the early 1820s, when the magistrates of Greenock were contemplating the state of the town's water supply, they must have been reading the lines in Samuel Taylor Coleridge's famous ballad *The Rime of the Ancient Mariner*, written in 1797. Although situated on the Clyde and provided with drinking water from the hills behind the town, Greenock did not have enough water to supply the needs of the town's growing manufacturing industries or domestic users. Along came Robert Thom, who, with the help of the Shaw's Water Company – an association set up by act of parliament in 1825 – engineered the 300-acre Loch Thom and 40-acre Compensation Reservoirs. An aqueduct, the Greenock Cut, was then channelled at 500ft above sea level to run six miles to the town. Completed in 1827 at a cost of £52,000, unlike the enterprise undertaken by the Ancient Mariner or some building projects of the modern era, it was never to be an albatross hanging round the neck of the taxpayer.

**ROUTE** From Glasgow take the M8/A8 road to Greenock, then the A78 Largs road to the Cornlees Bridge visitor centre car park, which is signposted. Start your walk turning left from the car park and gain the track running beside the small Compensation Reservoir until you reach Loch Thom Cottage. The track, climbing gently and steadily, becomes rough, but soon gives good views back over Loch Thom to the Hill of Stake and the Renfrewshire Hills. As the track climbs higher, the view north opens up over the Firth of Clyde to Helensburgh and the southern rim of the Highlands. Several kissing gates are negotiated before the path crosses a bridge and turns left at Overton, following the main Greenock Cut back to the start. The panorama on this stretch takes in the Cowal Peninsula, the Isles of Bute and the Cumbraes.

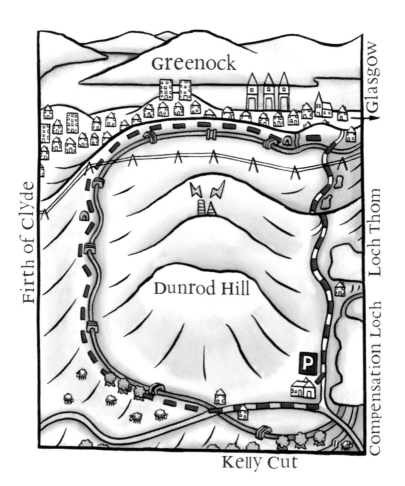

| MAP | OS Sheet 63, Firth of Clyde |
| --- | --- |
| **DISTANCE** | 7 miles (11km) |
| **RATING** | Moderate. Unmetalled road and tracks |
| **GEAR** | No need for special footwear |

# ST ANDREWS

Girded by the North Sea, St Andrews has survived storms, burnings and revolution to become what it is today: Scotland's Alma Mater. Its ancient university is consistently highly rated for its academic standards.

**THEMES** Ever since St Rule was washed ashore with the relics of St Andrew in the year 365 AD, St Andrews has been a place of Christian teaching, worship and martyrdom. Originally named Mucross – 'Promontory of the boars' – the town's name was changed, first to Kilrymont, 'Chapel of the King on the Mount', and then to Kilrule, 'Church of Rule', after St Rule converted the Picts to the Christian faith. The name Kilrule continued until the 9th century when the Picts finally succumbed to the Scots, who then gave the town the name of our patron saint. Founded in 1159, after a building programme spanning 160 years, the Cathedral of St Andrews was finally consecrated in the presence of King Robert the Bruce in 1318. Fire destroyed much of the cathedral in 1378 and a storm in 1409 knocked down the south

transept gable. Repairs were completed in 1440 and no further damage was done until the Reformation. In June 1559 a mob, inflamed by the preachings of John Knox, entered the cathedral and managed to destroy the labour of centuries in the course of a single day.

**ROUTE** Driving to St Andrews from the south, take the M90 to junction 8, then the A91 through Auchtermuchty and Cupar. If possible park in the car park in Golf Place, next to the Golf Museum and Sea Life Centre. Walk back past the museum and turn right into The Scores. This walkway to the long pier passes landmarks covering our Christian heritage from earliest times. There is the Martyrs' Monument, commemorating the Protestants executed prior to the Reformation, and the castle ruins, home to the bishops of St Andrews from 1200 AD; the cathedral and dedicated museum, housing the St Andrews sarcophagus carved by the Picts; and the ruined 12th century Culdee church, St Mary of the Rock, where the relics of St Andrew came ashore.

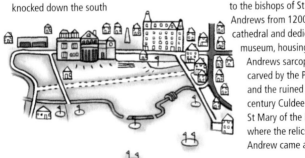

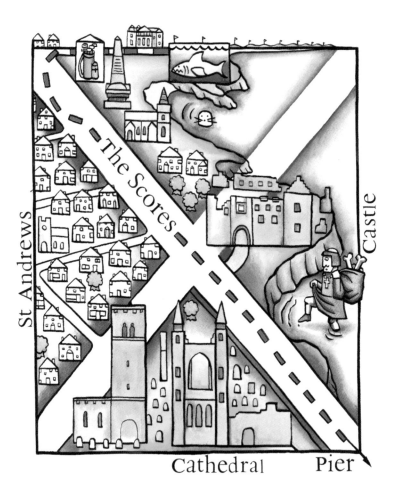

St Andrews

The Scores

Castle

Cathedral

Pier

| | |
|---|---|
| MAP | OS Sheet 59, St Andrews, Kirkcaldy & Glenrothes |
| DISTANCE | 2 miles (3km) |
| RATING | Easy. Pavements and walkways suitable for wheelchairs |
| GEAR | Shoes or trainers and a waterproof 'just in case' |

# RAILWAY RAMBLE, KILLIN

Engage any railway buff in a conversation about old lines and you might live to regret it. He's likely to prattle on happily for hours given the chance.

**THEMES** The demise of these scenic old routes is lamented by many, and the folly of closing them down is only now being recognised. Those that have survived, or even been resurrected through the efforts of enthusiasts, are benefiting from tourist income and are being promoted. For the lines that have gone – probably for good – it is not all doom and gloom. Enterprising local authorities have turned them in to leisure facilities for use by walkers, cyclists and horse riders. They make ideal paths and pass through some very attractive countryside. I have one on my own doorstep in Clackmannanshire, referred to in council-speak as a 'mixed leisure route'. This walk takes advantage of another two tracks – the Callander to Oban line and a spur that links it with the Stirlingshire village of Killin. It was built in the 1880s, the money coming from the local laird and local people. Both lines were closed in the autumn of 1965 after a rockfall in Glen Ogle.

**ROUTE** Start from the picturesque Falls of Dochart in Killin and leave the town in the direction of Crianlarich along the A827. Past a row of cottages, just before reaching the war memorial, look for a track on the left. Walk past two large houses to reach a gate. Go through it and bear right, following the railway trackbed under a bridge. Continue, climbing a gentle gradient through the trees. Pass Acharn farm to a point where the line joins a forest track. Continue to the A85 just above the Lix Toll junction. Cross the road with care and carry on along the track on the other side. It rises to reach Killin Junction station, where ruined station cottages and the former platform are still in evidence. This is where the branch line interesects with the Callander to Oban line. Our route transfers to the main line. Go left, up through the pines, to reach Glenogle Cottages. Just before them, a path on the left takes you to the road. Cross it to a car park and picnic area. A track runs through this to a gate, giving access to the next stage of our walk back towards Killin. After a couple of miles, turn right to a bridge over Achmore burn. Cross the bridge and continue to an exposed section of pipeline. Bear round to the left, staying with the forest track to arrive at a transmitter tower. Exit the forest through a gate. At the next junction turn left. A tarmac road goes through another gate and descends through the trees to meet up with the public road. Turn left to Killin.

| MAP | OS 51, Loch Tay |
| --- | --- |
| DISTANCE | 11 miles (18km) |
| RATING | Strenuous. Railway trackbed and forest tracks |
| GEAR | Boots and a waterproof |

# THE WHANGIE

The canyon formation of the Whangie has baffled geologists for generations. Was it caused by an earthquake, glacial plucking or just Auld Nick flicking his tail on the way to a witches' sabbath?

**THEMES** One of the more well-trodden routes due to its close proximity to Glasgow, the Whangie has also served as an ideal training ground for generations of the city's rock climbers. The strange geological formations offer a wide variety of modest height pitches which nevertheless demand considerable skill and agility from the climber. Over the years experts have argued about the exact process that formed the Whangie. Seismologists prefer the earthquake theory. Geologists prefer the phenomenon known as glacial plucking, where rock slabs are frozen into a glacial ice flow then plucked away and deposited further down the glacier. Mythologists, and those with vivid imaginations, favour the explanation that the cleft was formed when the Devil, thinking of forthcoming pleasures, was worked up into such a state of expectation that he lashed out his tail while flying over Stockie Muir, on his way to a witches' gathering.

**ROUTE** The walk starts from the large car park on the A809, halfway between Milngavie and Drymen, signposted Auchineden and Queen's View. The royal connection is with Queen Victoria, who relished touring the countryside. From the car park take the prominent path over the stone stile below the viewfinder indicator. A stairway of old railway sleepers protects the ground from excessive erosion at the start – always a problem on popular walks. Continue to climb uphill and cross a further stile at the top corner of the forest enclosure. Keeping to the lower path, close to the fence heading west, thread your way through small boulderfields to where the views open up across peat bogs, with Loch Lomond in the distance. As you continue west round the shoulder of the hill, the steeples and rock pinnacles of the Whangie soon make their dramatic impression as you come face to face with the fissure created by the Devil himself.

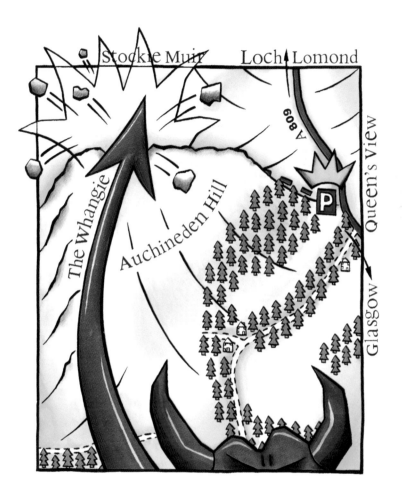

| MAP | Harvey's Glasgow Popular Hills or OS Sheet 64, Glasgow |
| DISTANCE | 3 miles (5km) |
| RATING | Easy. Path over moorland and boulderfields |
| GEAR | Stout footwear or well fitting trainers |

# BEN VENUE

It couldn't be a better place for a meeting of goblin folk. Straight out of Tolkien, Corrie na Urisgean, on the north side of Ben Venue, is reputedly the venue for all the goblins in Scotland to gather.

**THEMES** The Trossachs is often described as 'Scotland in miniature', the entire wider canvas of mountains, sparkling lochs and forests being mirrored in this compact and beautiful area. Hardly surprising, then, that it is a favourite with foreign visitors and Scots alike. With a much more enlightened policy dominating the forestry scene these days, and the move away from huge, impenetrable sitka spruce plantations, the landscape here is constantly evolving. Forest Enterprise, the government body which owns much of the woodland here, works hard to ensure everyone is made as welcome as possible to the national park. Great emphasis is laid on achieving an ecological balance of broadleaves and conifers. Walter Scott's links with the Trossachs are immortalised in the eponymous steamer which plies the length of Loch Katrine from April to October. Rob Roy, buried at Balquhidder churchyard, endures in Scots folklore and in movie culture with Liam Neeson in the starring role. On the north side of Ben Venue lies the Tolkienesque Corrie na Urisgean – corrie of the goblins – which is reputedly the meeting place for all the goblins in Scotland. For those with a vivid enough imagination it is not difficult to envisage such creatures living in this boulder-strewn place, surrounded by greenery, imbuing it with a sense of the supernatural.

**ROUTE** From Aberfoyle take the B829 and park opposite Ledard Farm on the shores of Loch Ard. Take the farm track between fields, then go left over a stile with a finger-post pointing the way to Ben Venue, following the line of the Ledard Burn. Not long into the walk a waterfall is reached, cascading into a pool. Scott, who stayed at Ledard working on his notes for *Rob Roy* and *Waverley*, is said to have sat here. The way ahead is along a path, which can be muddy in parts, winding its way upwards through dense birches. Emerging from the trees, the path crosses Ledard Burn and continues on the other side of a ladder stile. Soon you arrive at a broad bealach between Creag Tharsuinn and another outlier of Ben Venue, Beinn Bhreac. From here the path narrows, with superb views north over Loch Katrine. This stretch ends with a final pull up to the summit, with a few ups and downs in between. Although less than 2,400ft, Ben Venue feels higher and there is an unobstructed panorama from the top. Return by the same route.

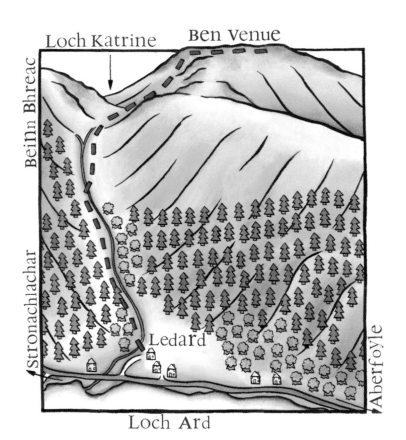

| MAP | OS 57 Stirling and Trossachs |
| --- | --- |
| DISTANCE | 6 mile round trip (10km) |
| RATING | Strenuous. Hill paths, which can be muddy in places |
| GEAR | Full hill-walking kit |

# ANSTRUTHER TO CRAIL

An easy saunter in the salt-sea air with scenic fishing villages to explore and some of the best fish and chips in Scotland to round it all off.

**THEMES** Anstruther, or 'Ainster' in local parlance, had a thriving fishing port until after the Second World War, when the decline in herring fishing led to its demise and that of some neighbouring harbours. It is one of the picturesque villages comprising the section of Fife coastline known as the East Neuk. Salt and coal were shipped from these ports and traded in return for riches from Europe. It's possible to walk all 78 miles of the coast, running from the Forth bridges to the Tay bridge at Newport on Tay. It offers some splendid coastal walking with thriving wildlife, strange rock formations carved by the sea, fossils and plenty of historic interest. The Dreel Burn, which separates Wester and Easter Anstruther, is celebrated in folklore. A sturdy beggar woman carried King James V across it to stop him getting his feet wet: her reward – a purse of gold. Crail, with its chocolate-box whitewashed cottages and their pantiled roofs and crow-stepped gables, is equally interesting. The tower of St Mary's kirk dates from the 13th century. Scratches and grooves in its stonework show where archers sharpened their arrow heads.

**ROUTE** Facing the Scottish Fisheries Museum opposite the harbour car park at Anstruther Easter, turn right and walk along the street, staying parallel to the sea front. Keep an eye open for intriguing details on the houses, which look as though they've been caught in a timewarp. Shore Street ends at a children's playground. Walk on eastwards, passing a caravan park. The Isle of May, five miles off shore, is visible out to sea and can be visited by boat from Anstruther in summer. It has the remains of a 12th-century monastery. The route is obvious and easy to follow as you progress, taking in the sights and sounds of the coast and the haunting cry of the curlew inland. The prominent landmark of Caiplie Coves is reached. This is a series of eroded sandstone pillars forming caves. The largest contains crosses carved into the walls, thought to date back to early Christian times. Follow the path to the right, further along passing the remains of a saltworks, dating back to around 1700. The path weaves between rocks to reach a line of steps on the left. Climb them and at the top Crail comes into view. In Crail, catch a bus back to Anstruther or return on foot. End the day with a feast of fish and chips from the shop in Anstruther.

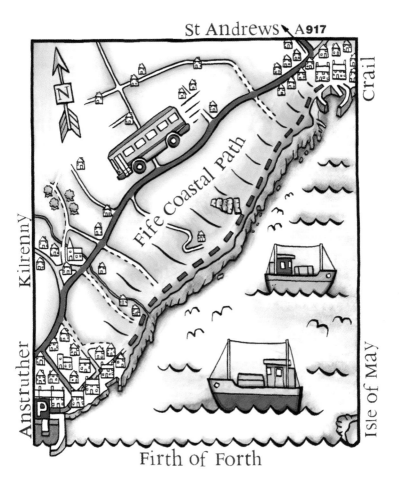

St Andrews A917

Crail

N

Fife Coastal path

Kilrenny

Anstruther

Isle of May

Firth of Forth

| MAP | OS 59 St Andrews |
|---|---|
| DISTANCE | 4 miles (6km) |
| RATING | Easy. Sea shore path |
| GEAR | Boots recommended, take a waterproof |

# BEN A'AN, TROSSACHS

The urge to bag a few Munros can sometimes be irresistible. But if your enthusiasm is over-ruling your fitness, test your stamina in the Trossachs before tackling the 3,000-footers.

**THEMES** The Trossachs have often been described as Scotland in miniature, and as a testing ground there can be no better place to start before engaging in more serious hillwalking pursuits. Being easily accessible from Scotland's central belt, the area offers all the joys of a mountain playground without the expense of overnight stays. Made famous as a tourist attraction as early as 1810 by Sir Walter Scott's epic poem *The Lady of the Lake*, the Trossachs gained notoriety 100 years earlier with the exploits of outlaw Rob Roy MacGregor, who used the area as a base for his cattle reiving activities. Originally the mountain valley between Loch Achray and Loch Katrine, the Trossachs now loosely include anything from the east shores of Loch Lomond to the town of Callander. The area also benefits from the attraction offered by its designation as Scotland's first National Park.

**ROUTE** Ben A'an by mountaineering standards is no expedition, but as with all hillwalking routes tackled in winter, needs treating with respect. If you are driving to the Trossachs via Aberfoyle, remember the A821 at the Duke's Pass is often closed during the winter months due to flooding or ice and snow. Check with the road authorities before setting off. Alternatively, take the M9 motorway to junction 10, then the A84 to Kilmahog, one mile past Callander. Turn off left along the A821 towards Aberfoyle. The Ben A'an car park is 200 yards past the castellated Tigh Mhor, formerly the Trossachs Hotel. With an army of boots pounding the route each year there should be no problem following the path, which starts opposite the car park. Cross the road with care. Shortcuts near the summit should be avoided, with the safest route winding around behind the main peak.

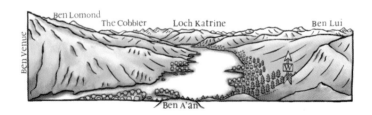

| MAP | OS 57, Stirling and Trossachs area |
|---|---|
| **DISTANCE** | 2 miles (3km) |
| **RATING** | Moderate. A short walk but strenuous in places |
| **GEAR** | Good footwear and windproof clothing essential |

# FETLAR, SHETLAND ISLES

Marauding Vikings have left their mark on Britain's most northerly land mass – a mosaic of more than 100 islands well worth visiting for keen ornithologists and walkers alike.

**THEMES** Fetlar means fertile land, and the island is known as the garden of Shetland. This walk takes in the Haltadans, one of the islands' surviving standing stone circles. Folklore has it that two stones within the outer circle represent a fiddler and his wife who were playing for a group of 'trows' – mythical, troll-like creatures invisible to the naked eye, who danced around the couple. As dawn broke they were all immortalised in stone. One of Shetland's oldest man-made structures is also encountered – the Finnigert Dyke. This Neolithic stone wall divides the island in two. At Leagarth House on the coast is Shetland's largest standing stone, the Stone of Ripples. Leagarth's original owner, Sir William Watson Cheyne, became one of the Victorian era's most famous surgeons, working with Lord Lister on the development of antiseptic surgery. At the Giant's Grave, local legend has it that a Norseman had his request fulfilled to be buried under his boat. Stones discovered in a rough boat shape have added substance to the folklore.

**ROUTE** From the ferry terminal at Oddsta on the north west corner of Fetlar, follow the road south to Brough Lodge, an unusual historic building. A short detour west gives a view out over the coast. Return and continue along the B9088 for around two miles, then turn north along the airstrip, with Skutes Water loch on the right, to enter the bird reserve. There's a fine view of the island and its neighbours from the summit of Voad Hill. There are archaeological sites to visit, including the Haltadans, described earlier, roughly linked in a heart shape on the map, before heading back along the airstrip to the road. Turn left and make for Leagarth House and the Ripple Stone. Continue east to Aithbank, a listed building. It's near here that the Giant's Grave is situated. A visit to the Fetlar Interpretive Centre rounds off the walk. It displays information on the wildlife, flora and geology of the island and has an extensive multi-media exhibition on Watson Cheyne, with photographs of the magnificent gardens that once encompassed his home.

For information on walks on Fetlar and the other Shetland Isles check the web pages at *www.visitshetland.com*.

Oddsta

Fetlar

B9088

Shetland Isles

| | |
|---|---|
| **MAP** | OS 1 Yell and Unst |
| **DISTANCE** | 8.5 miles (14km) |
| **RATING** | Moderate. Minor road, moorland and heath. Can be wet |
| **GEAR** | Full hill-walking kit |

# BEN VRACKIE

A resident herd of goats makes the wildlife interest on this walk unusual. They're harmless enough, but it's wise not to feed them or you'll be pestered!

**THEMES** The Victorian town of Pitlochry is one of Scotland's best-known holiday centres. For a relatively small place it boasts two distilleries, Blair Atholl and Edradour, Scotland's smallest. Both make fine malts and welcome visitors, offering guided tours. One of the town's most popular attractions is the dam and fish ladder, created during the Fifties when the River Tummel was harnessed for hydro-electric power. In the conservation village of Moulin, near the start of our walk, a church has stood for 1,400 years. Although the present structure is of fairly recent 19th century origin, the crusader's gravestone is evidence of earlier building on the site. From the summit of Ben Vrackie on a clear day it is possible to see Arthur's Seat in Edinburgh, Ben More on Mull and Ben Nevis. For walkers looking to extend their time out, it is possible to make a circuit of this route by continuing over Meall an Daimh and dropping down to Killiecrankie, returning to Pitlochry by the impressive Killiecrankie gorge. At the Soldier's Leap in the gorge, a trooper fleeing pursuers at the battle of Killiecrankie is said to have leaped across the River Garry – quite a feat when you see the gap, but his life was at stake after all.

**ROUTE** The A924 from Pitlochry to Braemar goes up through the village of Moulin. A small car park for the Ben Vrackie walk is signposted in Moulin. Work on the footpath has made this a much better walk under foot than it used to be. From the upper corner of the car park follow the path which keeps company with the Moulin Burn. It joins an estate track for a short distance then leaves it again to continue pleasantly through mixed woodland. A stile at the edge of the wood gives access to open moorland. The path curves gently uphill to the right with open views. It flattens out somewhat and rounds a corner to give a view of Loch a' Coire and the southern ramparts of Ben Vrackie, where the goats can often be seen making climbing look easy. Cross the dam wall and outflow and begin the fairly steep pull up to the summit. Since Ben Vrackie is less than 300ft short of Munro status there is a bit of work to do, but keep pegging steadily away. High up the path enters a corrie before the final push for the top, where a trig pillar and directional indicator disc await.

Ben Vracki

Erdradour

Moulin

Black Castle

Pitlochry **A9**

| | |
|---|---|
| MAP | OS 52 Pitlochry to Crieff and 43 Braemar |
| DISTANCE | 6 mile round trip (10km) |
| RATING | Strenuous. Tracks and paths |
| GEAR | Full hill-walking kit |

# STACKS OF DUNCANSBY

When the runners are the Boars of Duncansby or the Merry Men of Mey, a day at the races will leave you exhilarated without burning a hole in your pocket.

**THEMES** Duncansby Head marks the eastern entrance to the Pentland Firth, which, according to mariners both ancient and modern, is the most hazardous stretch of water on the British coastline. Between Duncansby Head and the Orkney Isles the tides can flow at rates up to 10 knots, causing dangerous tidal races known rather innocuously as the Merry Men of Mey and the Boars of Duncansby. During March, when the spring tides are met with high winds, the violence of the waves is phenomenal, when even the lighthouse windows have been known to be broken by rocks thrown up in the maelstrom from the shoreline, 220ft below. On clear, less turbulent days, the views across the firth to the Orkney Isles are outstanding, with the Old Man of Hoy, Britain's tallest sea stack and a haunt of rock climbers, peering over the cliffs on Hoy's western fringes.

**ROUTE** If travelling from the central belt, take the A9 north to Inverness then the A9/A99 north to Wick and on to John o' Groats. The final two miles to Duncansby Head are on a minor road heading east. Starting from the visitors' car park, look for a sign directing you along a path to the Stacks of Duncansby. After reaching the trig point, the path descends to the Geo of Sclaites – a sheer-sided cleft riven from the cliffs by the sea, which now form the natural nesting sites for many seabirds: puffins, razorbills, fulmars and arctic skuas, among others. The route, following the clifftop fence, first passes the Tom Thumb Stack, then the Peedie Stack (meaning little in local dialect), before going on to the Kiln of Flux to view the Muckle Stack. For a sight of the Pentland Firth at its most turbulent, time your visit when the tidal races are under starter's orders, five hours after Aberdeen's high tide.

Orkney Isles

Pentland Firth

Duncansby Head

John o'Groats

S

Stacks of Duncansby

| | |
|---|---|
| MAP | OS Sheet 12, Thurso Wick and surrounding area |
| DISTANCE | 2.5 miles (4km) |
| RATING | Easy. Cliff top path |
| GEAR | Strong footwear and windproof clothing |

# 22

# MEIKLE BIN

It could be no other place in the world. The trees are the Carron Valley Forest, the water the Carron Valley Reservoir, and Meikle Bin stands over them like a big brother.

**THEMES** In 1837, when the town fathers of Falkirk passed a byelaw that 'No person may wash tripe, potatoes, scullions or any other matter at the town wells,' little did the townspeople know it would be another 100 years before a sustainable, wholesome water supply would feed their needs. The Carron Valley Reservoir, opened in 1937 to satisfy the demand for water from the increasing population of Falkirk, is not only the area's public water supply but also a haven for the wildfowl and wildlife that surrounds its shores. This walk, starting from the picnic area below the Carron Dam, takes you along well-maintained forest roads to the summit of Meikle Bin, where excellent views can be had of the Carron and Forth Valleys, the Fintry and Ochil Hills and the mountains surrounding the Trossachs.

**ROUTE** At junction 5 of the M9, take the A872 towards Stirling. Fifty yards before the Bannockburn Heritage Centre, turn left, then sharp left again. This minor road leads you to a junction with the B818 at Carron Bridge. Turn right on to the B818. The picnic area is approximately one and a half miles along the road. The walk starts where a green barrier straddles the forestry road at the south east corner of the reservoir. Ignoring two roads that cut off to your left, follow this road to the south-east ridge of Meikle Bin, where a path leads up through trees to the summit trig point. Return the same way.

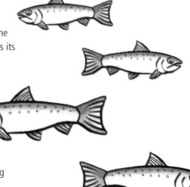

| | |
|---|---|
| **MAP** | OS Sheets 57, Stirling & Trossachs area and 64, Glasgow |
| **DISTANCE** | 8 miles (13km) |
| **RATING** | Moderate. Forestry road and paths |
| **GEAR** | Full hill-walking kit |

# 23

# BEN NEVIS

The king of Britain's mountains often has his head in the clouds, but on a clear day you can see for ever, so it seems.

**THEMES** At 4406ft and Britain's highest mountain, Ben Nevis throws down a challenge to all would-be mountaineers. The derivation of its name is obscure, possibilities being ugly mountain, venomous mountain, terrible mountain or – from 19th-century Gaelic commentators – mountain of the cold brow. In cloud for an average 300 days in the year, the summit of the Ben lies only a few hundred feet below the permanent snowline. The so-called 'tourist' track – which is the main route to the peak for walkers, mountain bikers, and in the past even a Model-T Ford – was built over 100 years ago to service the meteorological observatory, which sat at the top for more than 20 years. The observatory has lent its name to one of the great ridges that characterise the north-east face of the mountain. Together with a complex mass of precipitous gullies, corries and buttresses, they are the domain of climbers and mountaineers. Ben Nevis is especially well known for the quality and difficulty of its winter climbs, and some of the greatest names in British climbing history have honed their skills here in preparation for tackling the greater ranges of the world, including the Himalayas. Below the north-east face sits the CIC Hut, a climbing refuge erected

using funds from the parents of Charles Inglis Clark, who was killed in action in the First World War. The Ben Nevis race, held on the first Saturday in September, attracts up to 500 entrants annually. They tackle the arduous ascent to the top and back down again, with the best runners achieving times under an hour and a half. Most walkers take four hours for the ascent alone!

**ROUTE** From Fort William take the road into Glen Nevis, parking at the youth hostel. Do not be fooled by people who say this route, which starts after crossing the bridge opposite the hostel, is an easy climb. Starting from only 35ft above sea level, the track leading to the top is long and winding, with a five-to-one chance the Ben will have his head in the clouds once you get there. Not much reward, you'll agree, for a four-hour slog. But if, after climbing relentlessly upwards across aluminium bridges and past the half-way Lochan Meall an't Suidhe, you arrive at the summit with the whole of Britain below you, the scenery wrapped around you and blue skies above, the experience will never be forgotten. Take great care on misty days to follow the correct descent line, using a compass. Walkers deviating from it have lost their lives.

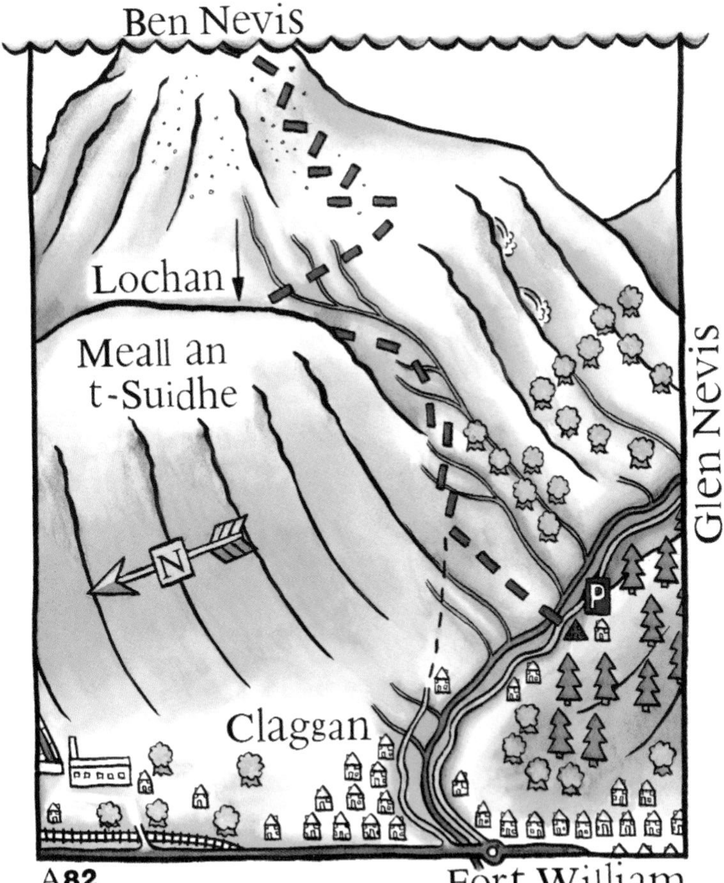

Ben Nevis

Lochan

Meall an
t-Suidhe

N

Claggan

Glen Nevis

P

A82

Fort William

| MAP | OS Sheet 41, Ben Nevis |
| --- | --- |
| DISTANCE | 7 miles (11km) |
| RATING | Strenuous. Rough mountain paths |
| GEAR | Full hill-walking kit |

# FALKIRK'S CALLENDAR PARK

Municipal parks are generally places walkers avoid, but away from the bouncy castles, pitch and putt and crazy golf, this one has some wilder territory to offer and provides an excellent family outing.

**THEMES** In 1783, when William 'Copper Bottom' Forbes bought the Barony of Callendar and Falkirk for £66,500, record has it that he produced a Bank of England £100,000 note and asked for change. Now completely refurbished by the local authority, the chateau-styled Callendar House is the focal point of the leisure park and grounds that surround it. The family mausoleum was commissioned on Forbes' death in 1815 by his second wife, Agnes Chalmers. It is an impressive building, 45ft high by 36ft in diameter, standing at the south-east corner of the park's artificial lake. Inhabiting the lake's islands is a variety of birdlife, while deer can often be spotted in the woods around the mausoleum. The park is well used by locals and visitors.

**ROUTE** Callendar Park is half a mile from Falkirk town centre, heading east out of the town towards Polmont and Linlithgow. Leave your car in the car park at the entrance to the estate and walk along the tree-lined avenue. Passing the pitch and putt and swing parks, you soon come to the north facade of Callendar House, where Mary Queen of Scots, Oliver Cromwell and Bonnie Prince Charlie have all been entertained. The house now boasts a museum, with an 18th-century working kitchen, a history research centre and much more. Walking past the house brings you to the lake and the Forbes Mausoleum, behind a walled enclosure. Continuing to circumnavigate the lake, along the grassy south bank, brings you to the lawns at the rear of Callendar House and a five-minute stroll back along the tree-lined avenue to the car.

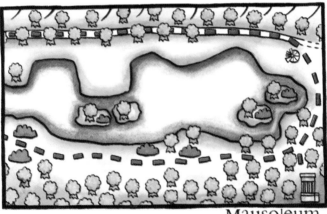

Mausoleum

| MAP | OS 65 and Callendar Park guide. |
|---|---|
| DISTANCE | 1.5 miles (2km) |
| RATING | Easy. A gentle stroll |
| GEAR | No special requirements |

# 25

# THE EILDON HILLS

Dominating the attractive town of Melrose, the three summits of the Eildons are a defining feature of the rural landscape that characterises the Scottish Borders.

**THEMES** Just like Edinburgh's Arthur's Seat, folklore has it that King Arthur and his knights lie sleeping beneath the Eildons, ready to wake in defence of Scotland. Where there are three hills now there was reputedly only one, before a wizard, Michael Scott, cleaved it apart. Geologists have a more prosaic explanation of their formation. Volcanic cores, they have remained prominent as the surrounding terrain has worn away. No one is sure when people first began living on the north hill of the Eildons, but by the time the Romans arrived in about 80AD there was a town of 300 huts and fortifications. It may have been headquarters to the Celtic tribe, the Selgovae. Mystery surrounds the demise of this settlement. It was abandoned for many centuries during the Iron Age, before the arrival of the Romans. Anyone there when they did arrive stood no chance against their military might and the Romans would have quashed any opposition before establishing the strategic garrison of Trimontium, named after the three peaks of the Eildons. Marking much later passages in the history of Scotland, a casket containing the heart of King Robert the Bruce is interred close to the walls of Melrose Abbey, where our walk starts and ends.

**ROUTE** From the car park at Melrose Abbey walk up Abbey Street to Market Square, with its old cross, and turn into Dingleton Road. Go under the bypass, keeping an eye out for a sign directing you left, between two houses. Ascend a made flight of steps up into the hills. Cross a stile, then continue along field edges, passing through three gates. Head for the saddle between the two hills, waymarked as the Eildon Hills walk, and ascend the hills as you wish. North Eildon has an Iron Age fort on its summit. On descent from North Eildon, link with a lower path that heads down through gorse. Go through a gate and follow an often muddy track between fences. Reaching the Bogle Burn road, turn right and in a short distance left down a lane. The A6091 bypass is crossed through an underpass. Go under the old railway bridge and immediately left on a wide path which curves right, down towards the west end of Newstead village. Follow the Eildon Walk signs half left, passing through a small stable on to a path which runs along a shelf with a fine view right of the River Tweed. Reaching the houses at Priorswalk continue along the road past an electricity sub-station. A path on the right leads through a small park back to Melrose Abbey.

Eildon Hills

A6091

Newstead

River Tweed

Melrose

Abbey

| MAP | OS 73 Peebles, Galashiels and surrounding area |
|---|---|
| DISTANCE | 5 miles (8km) |
| RATING | Moderate. Hill paths and road, can be muddy in places |
| GEAR | Full hill-walking kit, unless weather is very settled |

# 26

# FALLS OF CLYDE

Historically associated with Glasgow, ship building and industry, there is much more to the majestic River Clyde. This stretch in rural Lanarkshire has an abundance of wildlife and spectacular waterfalls.

**THEMES** The philanthropist Robert Owen engaged in a social experiment at New Lanark, believing his workers should live a decent lifestyle with fair conditions of employment. Alongside the village and mill buildings there, with a well-frequented visitor centre, is the Falls of Clyde wildlife reserve, managed by the Scottish Wildlife Trust. The Trust has a ranger centre based at the village and careful management of the area and its woodland is carried out. It is worth taking binoculars and a camera for the birdlife. Birds to look out for on the river are dippers, grey wagtails and, if you're fortunate, the elusive kingfisher. The badger population here is regularly monitored and the wildlife trust runs badger-watching sessions for those who want to see these rather shy creatures at close quarters. Of the three major waterfalls on the walk, Corra Linn is the most striking, especially when the river is in spate after a good downpour. Now in

ruins, Corra Castle is thought to be 500 years old. It was here that Martha Bannatyne pulled up the drawbridge to keep her future husband from going to the war.

**ROUTE** Start from the stone steps to the left of the visitor centre, alongside the nature reserve buildings. Climb the steps at the start of the walkway into the reserve, above Dundaff Linn waterfall. Continue along the boardwalk past Mill Dam, then turn right at a junction leading past Bonnington Power Station. Climb up steps to the Corra Linn viewpoint and have your camera at the ready. Moving on, the path goes up through woodland, high above the river gorge, and past Bonnington Linn. Cross the bridge above the weir and follow the footpath to the ruins of Corra Castle. Take the waymarked path past the castle and round the Corehouse Estate, past Corehouse Burn and a waterfall, before rejoining the outward route just south of the castle. Return along the outward route.

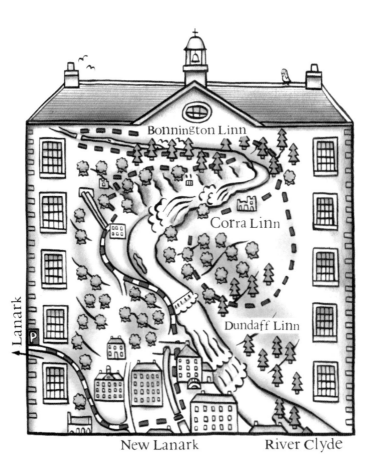

| **MAP** | OS Sheet 72, Upper Clyde Valley |
| **DISTANCE** | 6 miles (10km) |
| **RATING** | Moderate. Good paths and tracks. Care required on section between Bonnington Bridge and Corra Castle |
| **GEAR** | Walking boots and waterproofs in the wet. |

Bonnington Linn

Corra Linn

Dundaff Linn

Lanark

New Lanark

River Clyde

# 27

# LINLITHGOW TO COCKLEROY

A wee hill with big views, Cockleroy, standing above the historic Burgh of Linlithgow, provides a panorama stretching to Grangemouth and the Ochils.

**THEMES** Originally named Cuckold le Roi, after the alleged infidelity of a Scottish queen, Cockleroy has a dip on its summit known as Wallace's cradle or Wallace's bed. It is said to have given frequent shelter to the great William Wallace, knight from Elderslie. Although only 900ft above sea level, Cockleroy has outstanding views over the Firth of Forth and has long been the place to watch royal comings and goings in the district. Six thousand years ago, the nearby hill of Cairnpapple was a burial mound for local chiefs. More recently, on December 8, 1542, the royal birth of Mary Queen of Scots took place at nearby Linlithgow Palace.

**ROUTE** Although there is a car park just below the summit of Cockleroy, walking from Linlithgow gradually unlocks the countryside from the urban fringes of the town. Driving to the Royal Burgh from the east, leave the M9 motorway at junction three and turn left onto the A803, entering the town by the East Port. Two hundred yards after Linlithgow Cross, turn right and park in the Water Yett car park, near the health centre. From the car park walk back to the main street and turn right, heading west until you reach the Black Bitch public house. Cross the main street here and walk south up Preston Road. Go over the Union Canal, gradually leaving the urban sprawl of houses behind. Follow the road past the public water supply round to the Cockleroy car park, which is hidden in a thicket of pine trees on your right. The forestry road, at the west side of the car park, wends its way through an avenue of mature pines taking you to a stile which, when crossed, leads on to open moorland just below the summit.

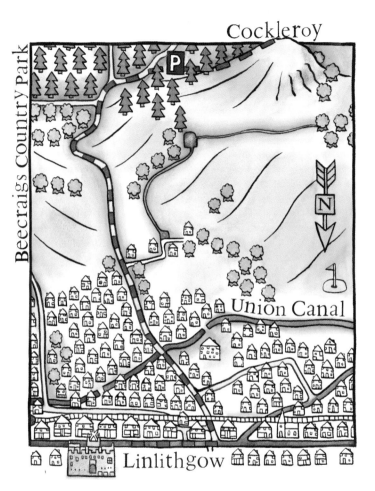

Cockleroy

Beecraigs Country Park

Union Canal

Linlithgow

| MAP | OS Sheet 65, Falkirk and West Lothian |
|---|---|
| DISTANCE | 4 miles (6km) |
| RATING | Easy. Country roads and open moorland |
| GEAR | Outdoor wear, stout shoes recommended |

# 28

# TINTO HILL

The Hill of Fire – an ancient site of sacrificial burial and sun worship, and when the sun is up the view from the top is well worth the sacrifice of getting there.

**THEMES** Maps are fascinating things. Like books they provide hours of interest for lovers of the outdoors. Ordnance Survey Sheet 72 is no exception, and the names are a delight. We get Fatlips Castle, Turkey Hill and the Deil's Barn Door to name but a few.

Tinto Hill dominates the landscape east of Lanark. The large Bronze Age cairn on the summit, which measures 150ft wide by 20ft high, is said to have been built by stones carried to the top by locals as a penance. Whatever the sins of our forefathers, the views, as they unburdened themselves at the top, must have come as a blessing.

On a clear day, 60 miles to the south, across the English border in the Lake District, Skiddaw can be seen. Thirty miles north, crowning the Ochils, is Ben Cleuch. Goat Fell on Arran rises from the Clyde, 60 miles to the west, while looking east towards Peebles, Dun Rig is 20 miles away.

**ROUTE** The start of this walk is three miles east of Lanark on the A73. Park in the car park at Fallburn, which has been set aside for walkers, near the Thankerton crossroads. The farm shop and tearoom is an added bonus for your return. At the car park, go through a kissing gate and follow the track uphill, passing the prehistoric Fallburn Fort, after crossing a stile. The steep gravel track soon takes you over the top of Totherin Hill before the final ascent to the summit cairn of Tinto. From the summit, this circular route turns right, heading west, down over Lochlyoch Hill to the forestry plantation at Howgate Mouth. Turning right, as you cross a fence at the bottom, follow the track past Howgate Farm. Another right turn, three-quarters of a mile after the farm, signals the final stage of your walk along three miles of lightly used rural road, to that well earned rest at the tearoom.

| | |
|---|---|
| **MAP** | OS Sheet 72, Upper Clyde Valley |
| **DISTANCE** | 7.5 miles (12km) |
| **RATING** | Moderate. Moorland tracks, returning by road |
| **GEAR** | Waterproof clothing and strong footwear |

# 29

# SCHIEHALLION

The John Muir Trust owns the eastern side of this fine Perthshire landmark and the well-worn footpath to the summit has been greatly improved.

**THEMES** An excellent outing both for Munro-baggers, and walkers simply intent on climbing a splendid hill, Schiehallion – fairy hill of the Caledonians – became a victim of its own popularity. Over the years, the path from the car park at Braes of Foss had become badly eroded under the pounding of walking legions. With Scotland's mountains sometimes bought and sold as if they were being traded at the Glasgow Barras, it's good to know that at least this one is in safe hands. Conservation body the John Muir Trust raised £300,000 to cover the purchase of the eastern half of Schiehallion and the cost of erosion repairs. Net surfers can visit the trust's website for a history of the project and the trust's other activities and achievements. Contained in a National Scenic Area and remarkable for its limestone pavement and associated plantlife, the mountain is notable in another respect. Experiments were conducted here in the 18th century by astronomer royal Nevil Maskelyne to measure the Earth's mass. More importantly for walkers, it also gave rise to the development of land surface contour lines – now universally used on maps – because points of equal height on the mountain were marked.

**ROUTE** About four miles south of Tummel Bridge, take the narrow road that branches off the B846 and skirts a stand of forestry to arrive at a car park at the extreme western end of the plantation. From here the standard route is easily followed up the eastern shoulder of Schiehallion. A plaque at the forestry car park, set up in 1982 on the 250th anniversary of Maskelyne's birth, commemorates the experiments he conducted. At first the path crosses grassy moorland towards the bottom of the ridge, then begins to rise over peaty ground where the worst erosion has occurred. Higher up the terrain becomes much firmer and stony, making the walking easier under foot even if the stops for breath are more frequent! Closer to the 1,083ft summit there are quartzite boulders, providing handy niches to shelter from the wind and enjoy a well-earned snack. More adventurous walkers who prefer to do their own thing, and the mountain a favour at the same time, can ascend the western ridge, either by following the Tempar Burn or, from Braes of Foss, skirting the southern slopes along the line of the Allt Mor river, eventually accessing the ridge.

| MAP | OS 51 Loch Tay |
|---|---|
| DISTANCE | 6 mile round trip (10km) |
| RATING | Strenuous. Mountain path, rocky higher up |
| GEAR | Full hill-walking kit |

# 30

# BEINN EIGHE, TORRIDON

At the heart of Britain's first National Nature Reserve, Beinn Eighe is one of Scotland's finest hills by any standards, in an area with more than its fair share of striking peaks and scenery.

**THEMES** Glinting in sunlight, the white quartzite blocks on the summit ridges of this Torridonian giant make it look from a distance as if it's snow-capped all year round. Beneath the quartzite lie some of the oldest rocks in the world. The base layer of Lewisian Gneiss dates back 1,600 million years, topped by a layer of distinctive red Torridonian sandstone around half as old. Dramatic is an over-used adjective in the context of mountains, but it is amply justified to describe this beautiful corner of western Scotland – a veritable paradise for wildlife. More than 130 varieties of birds have been recorded, among them some of Britain's rarest, including the golden eagle and red- and black-throated divers in the lochs. Those who forsake their cars and venture into the wilds here will be rewarded by the sight of many a hidden scenic gem. In the case of Beinn Eighe it is the towering triple buttress of tongue-twisting Coire Mhic Fhearchair (corry vic erracher is a reasonable pronunciation) which stands out. The corrie is encountered on our walk. Other mountains will beckon too, and for those intimidated by the heights there is plenty of lower territory to explore.

**ROUTE** A parking place on the narrow road that runs between Torridon and Kinlochewe is the starting place. It is located between Beinn Eighe and Liathach, near the bridge over the Allt a Choire Dhuibh Mhor burn. From here follow the path that heads up between the two mountains alongside the burn. A lochan on the left and a large cairn mark the point of departure from the main path. Take the subsidiary path right, which rounds Sail Mhor into Coire Mhic Fhearchair. The coire and its lochan are hidden until the last moment. Ascending beside a waterfall, the scene suddenly bursts on the eye. Take the lochan's right-hand side and make for the bealach under Ruadh-stac Mor, Beinn Eighe's highest point and a Munro. Backtrack to the bealach and follow the ridge left to Spidean Coire nan Clach, another summit, promoted to Munro status in the latest update. Taking care, descend south via Stuc Coire an Laoigh into Coire an Laoigh and pick up the path which weaves down alongside the Allt Coire an Laoigh burn to the road. Then it's a plod back to the car park. Those who prefer can return by the outward route after viewing Coire Mhic Fhearchair, for a shorter, less arduous day.

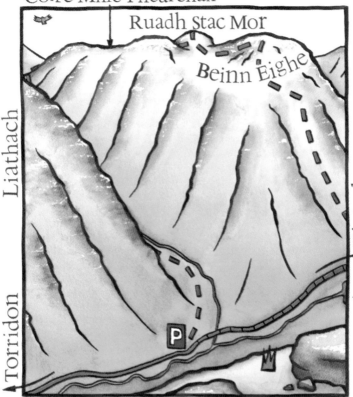

Coire Mhic Fhearchair

Ruadh Stac Mor

Beinn Eighe

Liathach

Torridon

Kinlochewe

A896

Sgurr Dubh

| | |
|---|---|
| **MAP** | OS Outdoor Leisure Map, The Cuillin and Torridon Hills |
| **DISTANCE** | 9 miles (14km) |
| **RATING** | Strenuous. Mountain and moorland paths |
| **GEAR** | Full hill-walking kit |

# 31

# BIRNAM HILL

It may be minor in stature at only just over 1,300ft, but this hill – and especially the woodland surrounding it – is well known for its significance in literary history.

**THEMES** 'Macbeth shall never vanquish'd be until Great Birnam Wood to High Dunsinane Hill shall come against him.' So runs the fateful prophecy delivered to Macbeth, in one of Shakespeare's most potent tragedies, by an apparition conjured up by the 'black and midnight hags', who fuel his fantasies of grandeur, and lead ultimately to death at the hands of Macduff, who was not 'of woman born' and therefore able to slay Macbeth. The Birnam Oak, ancient and only barely standing with a little help from supports these days, is said to be the last survivor of the wood from which soldiers cut branches in the year 1057 to use as camouflage on their way to do battle at Dunsinane Hill, 12 miles away.

For such a small community, Birnam is not found wanting when it comes to literary connections. Although more closely associated with the Lake District, Beatrix Potter spent happy childhood summers at Dalguise House, near Dunkeld, between 1871 and 1881. It was while staying at Eastwood in Dunkeld that she was inspired to write *Peter Rabbit*. Birnam Institute houses a Beatrix Potter exhibition and nearby is a commemorative garden with sculptures taken from the books.

**ROUTE** From the railway station car park in Birnam village, go under the railway and turn left along a minor road, passing large detached houses. After Creagmor, the last house on the left, the metalled surface becomes a rough track. A turning circle is reached with a way marker indicating the route. Stroll through the lovely broadleaved woodland skirting the base of Birnam Hill with the railway line to your left. Rounding a house called Creagbeithe, the path continues to follow the railway, then begins to climb. At the point where a seat provides a view across Dunkeld and the Tay, turn right. Follow the path to a quarry and continue walking to a signposted path going uphill to the right. Walk on uphill, eventually reaching a sign saying King's Seat. Don't take the branch path, but head on towards the junction for Stair Bridge. Make a short diversion to the bridge for a spectacular view, then retrace your steps to the main path for the final push to the summit, marked by a large cairn. Having enjoyed a well-earned rest and taken in the vista over the surrounding countryside, head due north to leave the top and descend along a meandering path down the hill again, following the waymarkers. Finally, turn right along Inchewan Burn to reach the station and the car park.

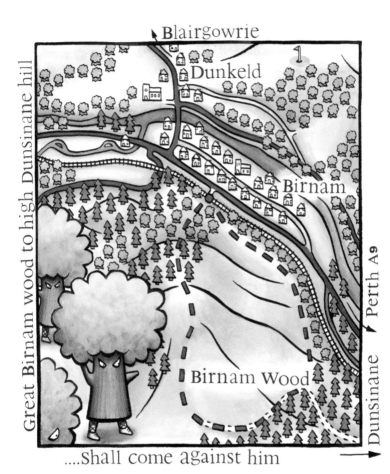

| MAP | OS 52 Pitlochry to Crieff |
|---|---|
| DISTANCE | 5 miles (8km) |
| RATING | Moderate. A minor road, paths and tracks |
| GEAR | Walking boots and waterproofs |

# 32

# DUN CAAN

Its truncated shape allows this Raasay hill to be spotted easily from miles away on Skye. A ferry journey from Sconser adds to the anticipation of the walk and makes for an entertaining outing for anyone visiting the north west.

**THEMES** The traveller James Boswell is said to have danced a jig of pleasure on the flat-topped summit of Dun Caan. Standing there with a seascape on one side and views back to the Skye Cuillin on the other, it's easy to understand why. Raasay is a fascinating island on which to spend the day, or longer. The scenery can be literally breathtaking, there is abundant wildlife and some very rare flora on the island's east coast. Birthplace of the Gaelic poet Sorley MacLean, Raasay was home to German prisoners during the First World War. They were put to work mining iron ore and the remains of the workings can still be seen. Many of them died during an influenza epidemic in 1918 and were buried on Raasay. Fifteenth-century Brochel Castle lies to the north. Built by invaders from the outer Hebrides, it later became home to the clan chiefs of the MacLeods of Raasay. After the notorious defeat of the Highlanders at Culloden, Bonnie Prince Charlie found refuge for a time in a shepherd's cottage on the island. In retaliation, and presumably in hope of flushing him out, government troops burnt every house to the ground.

**ROUTE** Take the ferry from Sconser – an early one is advised to make sure of getting back before the last one of the day from Raasay. After disembarking at East Suisnish make your way straight over the hillside ahead, keeping the old iron ore furnaces on your right. Follow the dismantled railway used by the miners in a north-easterly direction across open ground, enjoying views back to Skye. Cross a stile into a forestry plantation and continue to a small gorge, which is spanned by the remains of a railway viaduct. Go down in to the gorge, up the other side and continue in the same direction to the edge of the plantation. Cross a stile, then go over the road which leads down to Inverarish. Carry on across a bridge through another plantation and out on to open ground. A path, sometimes boggy, climbs steadily alongside the Inverarish Burn. It eventually enters a wild and beautiful area passing Loch na Mna to the edge of Loch na Meilich under Dun Caan. Veer right and climb the well-worn route to the summit. Return the same way.

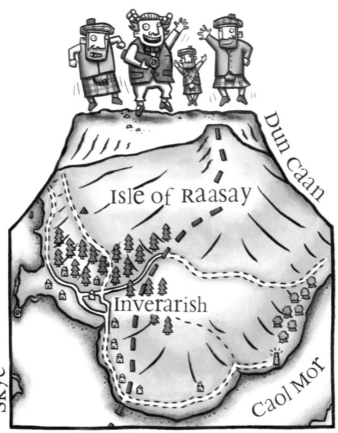

| MAP | OS 32 South Skye |
| --- | --- |
| **DISTANCE** | 8 miles (13km) |
| **RATING** | Strenuous. Rough paths, boggy in places |
| **GEAR** | Full hill-walking kit |

# 33

# LOCH AN EILEIN

The gentle circuit round this little loch – a jewel in the majestic crown of the Cairngorms – offers plenty of interest, and there's legend too, surrounding a ruined castle.

**THEMES** The Caledonian pinewoods that form the forest of Rothiemurchus once covered swathes of Scotland in the days of the great Forest of Caledon. They are a haven for wildlife and there is no richer source of it than here, around Loch an Eilein. Some of Britain's rarest birds inhabit this place: the giant, turkey-like capercaillie, the lively, restless siskin and the native Scottish crossbill, deriving its name from its crossed beak, designed for prising seeds from pine cones. Ospreys sometimes fish on this loch, but to be sure of seeing them you'll need to visit the RSPB reserve and visitor centre at nearby Loch Garten. Go on the steam train from Aviemore and make a day of it. Eilein translates as island, and on the one in this loch sits a ruined fortress dating back to the 14th century. Its slightly sinister ambience is perhaps no accident, for it is believed to have been the lair of Alexander Stewart, the outlawed son of the Scots king Robert II. A warlord and bandit, he became known as the Wolf of Badenoch after burning down Elgin cathedral in 1390 in retaliation for the bishop's criticism of his private life.

**ROUTE** About a mile south west of Inverdrui, on the B970 to Feshiebridge, a minor road leads to a car park at the northern end of Loch an Eilein. Head right from the car park, passing the informative visitor centre. Stroll through the pinewoods on the western side of the loch with the ruined, photogenic castle in view. A line of stepping stones which gave access to it can still be seen when the loch is low. Listen and watch for wildlife. Continue past a clearing with Loch an Eilein cottage. Reaching the south western corner of the loch turn left and go up a low bank, veering away from the loch shore. In a short while cross the footbridge over the burn between Loch Gamhna and Loch an Eilein. The path rejoins the lochside for a time and then, at an inlet on the corner of a headland, forsakes it once more. Continue to a path junction where there is a seat. Turn left and follow the track back to the start.

| MAP | OS 36 Grantown, Aviemore and Cairngorm area |
|-----|---------------------------------------------|
| DISTANCE | 3 miles (7km) |
| RATING | Easy. Forest and lochside paths |
| GEAR | Boots recommended, and a waterproof |

# 34

# AROUND LOCH TROOL

Loch Trool is a liquid gleam in a magnificent glen, well known to discerning walkers in the south of Scotland. Woods and crags surrounding the loch add to the beauty, and the scenery is reminiscent of the Trossachs or the English Lake District.

**THEMES** Tradition has it that in 1307 followers of Robert the Bruce, positioned high above the loch on the southern slopes of Glen Trool, trundled rocks on to an English force led by the Earl of Pembroke. The resulting rout apparently turned the tide in Bruce's favour after a period when things had not been faring well for him in his conflict with the English. He had been defeated at Methven and fled to Ireland, where his famous encounter with the spider in the cave on Rathlin Island took place, which spurred him to try again in his power struggle. The Loch Trool incident is marked by the Bruce's Stone on the other side of the loch. The Martyrs' Tomb, near the start of this walk, is another symbol of turbulence in Scottish history – this time religious, stemming from the 1558 Reformation. It led to rebellion and an edict by Charles II that non-conformist ministers should be removed from office.

The tomb commemorates the occasion on January 25, 1685 when six non-conformist Covenanters, as they were called, were caught praying and executed for not adhering to the 'official' religion.

**ROUTE** Start from the Caldons campsite at the western end of the loch. A short, signed spur path leads to the Martyrs' Tomb. Beyond the campsite shop take the road on the left, heading towards the loch. A Southern Upland Way signpost with its thistle logo points the way across a small bridge. After crossing the bridge either follow the track down to the lochside or continue with the upland way route – easier walking but less scenic. The two routes join beyond a little spur of land jutting into the loch and the path continues to an area of flat flood plain at the eastern end of the loch. Walk on past forestry on the right to a bridge crossing Glenhead Burn. Go over the bridge and make a left turn along the Glenhead Farm track, now on the return route. Passing Buchan House, a sharp bend leads to the Bruce's Stone car park. Continue along the road below the Fell of Eschoncan and past the entrance track to Glen Trool Lodge. Not far beyond this the Pulnabaich Burn is reached and a signposted path leaves the road on the left and winds through trees back to the start.

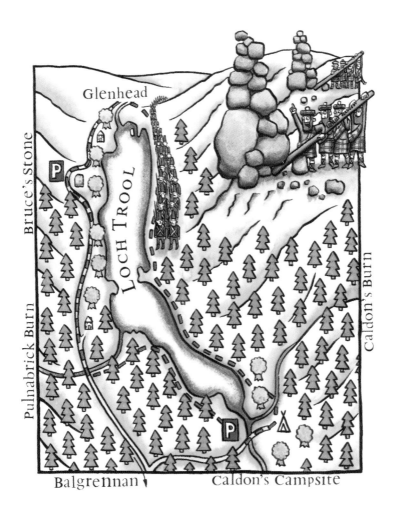

| **MAP** | OS Sheet 77 or Harvey's Galloway Hills |
| **DISTANCE** | 5 miles (8km) |
| **RATING** | Easy. Good paths and tracks |
| **GEAR** | Trainers fine in dry weather but walking boots advised |

# 35

# LARGO LAW

A visit to the East Neuk of Fife's village of Largo, washed by the Firth of Forth and dried by its sea breezes, reveals a slow and dignified way of life.

**THEMES** Largo was the birthplace of Alexander Selkirk, whose life story was the inspiration for Daniel Defoe's classic story *Robinson Crusoe*. A statue to Selkirk can be seen set in to the wall above two doorways in the town. Largo has long been the home of famous sailors. Probably the most distinguished of its seafaring sons was Admiral Andrew Wood, friend of the Stewart Kings James III and IV. In 1498 Wood fought a sea battle against the English around the Isle of May, capturing three English ships and their commander, Admiral Stephen Bull. For his services, James IV presented Wood with the Lands of Largo. Once known as the 'Hill of the Britons', Largo Law is the most prominent landmark on the East Neuk of Fife's flat coastland.

**ROUTE** Take the A915 from Kirkcaldy, first to Lower then to Upper Largo. Shortly before the A915/A917 junction, a minor road turns off to the left. Follow this road to Kirkton of Largo primary school and park in the car park north of the school. From there go through a kissing gate following the signs directing you on to the hillside via Chesterstone Farm. A frontal assault of Largo Law, directly up the south face, leads you to a false summit where a 50ft descent and final scramble about 60ft takes you to the summit cairn and trig point, where the views are magnificent. First look south across the Firth of Forth to Edinburgh, then trace the coastline east, following it out to the North Sea and round into the Firth of Tay to Dundee. Nestling between the two cities is the whole of the Kingdom of Fife.

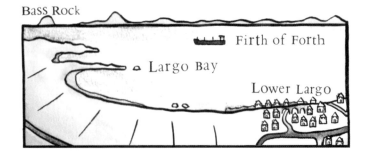

# AROUND ARTHUR'S SEAT

Edinburgh's most prominent and well-loved landmark is a designated world heritage site and draws both locals and tourists to it like a honeypot.

**THEMES** Holyrood Park, used for centuries for religious, defensive and recreational purposes, achieved its status as a royal park in the 16th century. Extending to 650 acres and a hunting ground for past monarchs, it is in the ownership of the Crown. These days it provides the capital's inhabitants with a jealously-guarded source of fresh air and exercise. Joggers, walkers, tourists and lovers whispering sweet nothings into each other's ears make full use of a resource which must surely be the envy of city dwellers elsewhere. The sense of wildness comes largely from the volcanic eminence of Arthur's Seat, ringed on its western side by the imposing Salisbury Crags, acting as a natural barrier to the bustle of the city. Legend has it that deep in the bowels of the hill, King Arthur and his knights slumber, ready to wake and come to Scotland's aid in battle. To the south of Arthur's Seat is the rural village of Duddingston with its attractive loch. It was the setting for Sir Henry Raeburn's famous portrait of the Rev Robert Walker skating. The painting is now in the National Gallery. Duddingston, with its country atmosphere, could not be a greater contrast to Edinburgh. It has been a conservation area since 1975, and has a 12th century church and the

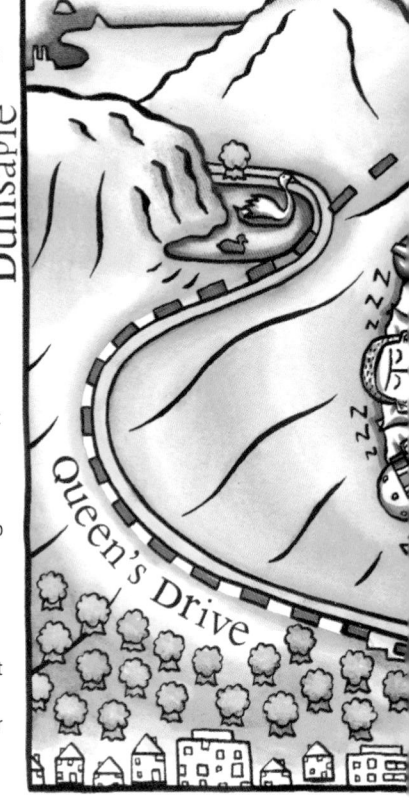

Sheep Heid Inn – a watering hole which vies for the title of the oldest licensed premises in Scotland. The Innocent ●●●●

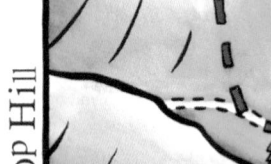

West Lomond

Falkland

Bishop Hill

Glenrothes

Loch Leven

| MAP | OS 58 Perth to Alloa |
|---|---|
| DISTANCE | 5 miles (8km) |
| RATING | Moderate. Moorland paths |
| GEAR | Full hill-walking kit |

# WEST LOMOND

Not to be confused with their much bigger namesake towering above Loch Lomond, the Lomonds of Fife offer much easier ascents but can still give a feeling of remoteness in an area with many historical connections.

**THEMES** Prominent when viewed from the summit of West Lomond, and visible on the ascent up to it, is Loch Leven. One of Europe's largest wildfowl sanctuaries, it offers a wintering haven for thousands of geese and ducks – notably pinkfoot and greylag geese – which can be seen, and heard, returning to the loch in their great V-shaped skeins each autumn. It's a definite sign that the seasons are on the change. The excellent RSPB reserve on the shores of the loch is well worth a visit. Loch Leven has seven islands, the biggest of them St Serf's, with its 9th-century priory. Mary Queen of Scots was imprisoned in a tower on Castle Island in 1568. She made good her escape with the help of Willy Douglas, who locked her guards in the Great Hall and threw the keys into the loch. Incredibly, 300 years later the keys were found. At the heart of the medieval village of Falkland is Falkland Palace, a country residence and hunting lodge of the Stuart monarchs, constructed between 1501 and 1541. A fine example of Renaissance architecture, it has an ornate chapel and is surrounded by internationally renowned gardens. Its Royal Tennis Court is reputedly the world's oldest and is still in use today.

**ROUTE** Take the minor road that runs between the villages of Leslie and Falkland and park at Craigmead. A gate at the back of the car park takes you to a stile. Cross this and follow the grassy track that joins another coming from the right. Continue straight ahead over the open moorland. The track eventually divides. Ignore a narrower path forking to the right and stay with the main path, making for West Lomond, the highest point in Fife at 1,712ft. The views are extensive. From the summit descend to the south west and double back left under the hill on a narrowish path beside a stone wall. Cross a stile and take the easiest line down to a corner between stone walls alongside the Lothrie Burn. Cross a stile and continue to a gate giving access to woodland. The low dam containing Harperleas Reservoir is reached. Go through a gate and follow the path under the dam. Continue past a ruined manor house, Ballo Castle, to a track. Turn right and continue on the track past the entrance to Little Ballo farm and a small plantation on the right. The track turns left and emerges on the road leading back to Craigmead. Turn left and in a short distance arrive at the car park.

Sgorr nam Fhiannaidh

The Pap of Glencoe

Glencoe

A82

Loch Leven

Glencoe

| | |
|---|---|
| **MAP** | OS 41, Ben Nevis |
| **DISTANCE** | 5 miles (8km) |
| **RATING** | Moderate. Grass and heather, then a rocky scramble |
| **GEAR** | Full hill-walking kit |

# SGORR NA CICHE: THE PAP OF GLENCOE

Cruel was the snow that swept Glencoe, but more cruel the foe that murdered the house of MacDonald.

**THEMES** In 1691, William III published a proclamation to all Highlanders loyal to King James VII to accept an amnesty and swear an oath of allegiance to his government. MacIan, chief of the clan MacDonald of Glencoe, after being refused the oath at Fort William on December 31 – the last day allowed under the proclamation – had to wait, through no fault of his own, until January 6 to swear allegiance at Inveraray. The ruling powers thought this breach of the deadline was the perfect excuse to set an example to the clans. By a chain of command running down from King William, through the Secretary of State for Scotland, Sir John Dalrymple, Captain Robert Campbell of Glen Lyon was ordered to march his troops against the rebels and destroy them by fire and sword. Campbell, under a parole of honour, came with no hostile intentions, arriving in Glencoe with 120 Redcoats at the beginning of February. After being welcomed according to the best traditions of Highland hospitality, Campbell turned on his hosts, at five o'clock, on the morning of February 13, 1692, slaughtering 38 men and boys, with an unspecified number of women and children dying of exposure as they attempted to escape the glen through violent snowstorms.

**ROUTE** Sgorr na Ciche, or the Pap of Glencoe, situated at the extreme west of the famous glen, is one of the great landmark hills of the area. Take the A82 north from Crianlarich to Glencoe village and park there. Walking the mile along to the start, follow the road to the Bridge of Coe and turn right, keeping the forest on your left. At the end of the forest there is a kissing gate, leading through cattle pens. Access on to the hill is along a rough service track. Where the track forks, keep right to cross the burn, taking the path up the obvious gully to the col between the Pap and the ridge along to Sgorr nam Fiannaidh. From the col, a rough scramble leads to the 2,434ft summit.

Ayr

Burns Cottage

The Tam O' Shanter Experience

Alloway

River Doon • Kirk Alloway

Brig o' Doon

| MAP | OS Sheet 70, Ayr and Kilmarnock |
|---|---|
| DISTANCE | 4 miles (6km) |
| RATING | Easy. A walk round Burns National Heritage Park |
| GEAR | A clove of garlic and your imagination |

# THE BURNS TRAIL

When chapman billies leave the street,
And drouthy neebors, neebors meet –
It's time to go and face the gale,
An' walk the famous bardie's trail.

**THEMES** When a stormy gust of 1759 blew down the west gable of the newly built Burns Cottage, not many people would have given the building much chance of surviving the winter, far less another 240 years. Nevertheless, due to the poetic genius of the son, rather than the civil engineering skills of the father, survive the 'Auld Clay Biggan' did, giving people today a chance to share in the unique atmosphere of our national bard's birthplace. Robert Burns was feted far and wide during his lifetime, but no better accolade could be given to his work than the universal recognition his poetry and songs receive during the annual New Year celebrations, with Auld Lang Syne taking centre stage as the international dateline takes its midnight stroll around the globe.

**ROUTE** The walk round the Burns National Heritage Park in Alloway, near Ayr, follows the hoofprints of Tam o' Shanter's grey mare Meg, and walkers would do well to keep their wits about them. From the Burns Cottage car park, take a left, then right, on to Monument Road, (Kirk Alloway is drawin' nigh, whare ghosts and houlets nightly cry; By this time you'll hae crossed the ford, whare in the snaw the chapman smoor'd; pass the birks and the meikle stane, whare drunken Charlie brak's neck bane; and thro' the whins, and by the cairn, whare hunters fund the murdered bairn; and near the thorn, above the well, whare Mungo's mither hang'd hersel.) After passing Kirk Alloway, the setting for Tam o' Shanter's famous 'dance o' witches', a turn to your left takes you down to the Auld Brig o' Doon, where Tam won his race to the keystane o' the brig, by a tail.

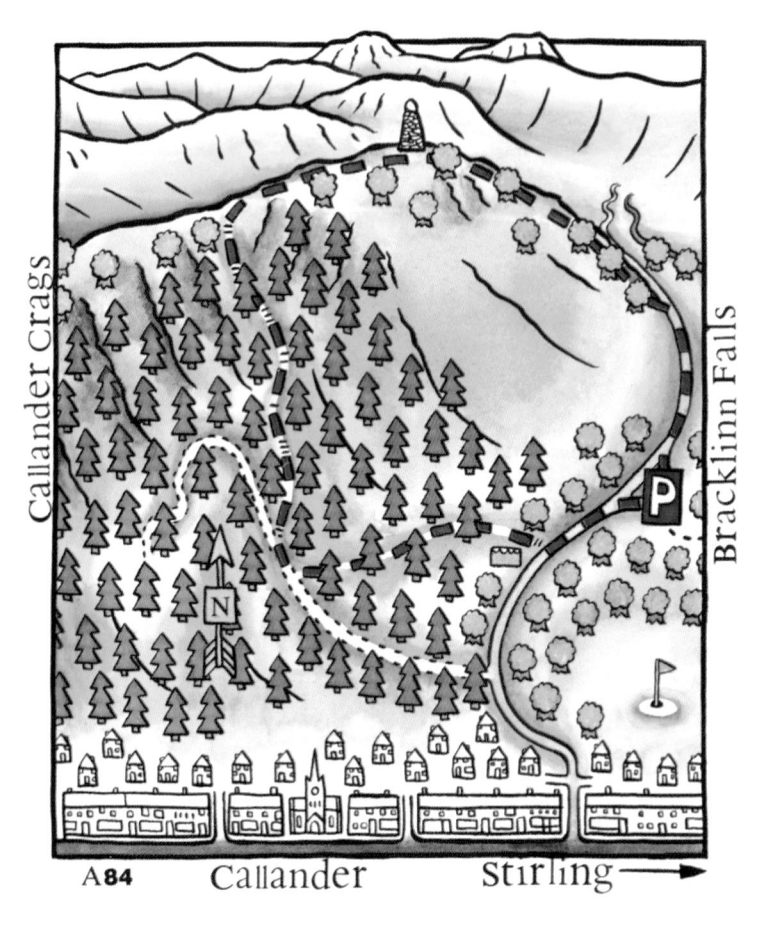

| MAP | OS Sheet 57, Stirling & Trossachs area |
| --- | --- |
| DISTANCE | 2 miles (3km) |
| RATING | Moderate. Steep in places. A few boggy areas in the wet |
| GEAR | Walking boots and waterproofs |

# CALLANDER CRAGS

The Perthshire town of Callander has many attractions for the collector of Highland souvenirs, but a scramble up the Crags, which form the town's backdrop, will stay golden in the memory long after the gilt on the trinkets has faded.

**THEMES** On September 1, 1869, when Queen Victoria passed through Callander, she described it as: "A one street town with very few shops." A lot has changed since that visit. The population has increased to over 3,000 and the main street has been handed over to shopkeepers servicing the needs of the many thousands of tourists visiting this attractive Perthshire town. Rising 1000ft above the town, Callander Crags look inaccessible to all but the most experienced technical climbers, but beneath the trees there are amenable paths wending their way uphill to the summit cairn, built in 1897 to commemorate Victoria's Diamond Jubilee. The lovely Trossachs landscape is closely linked with Sir Walter Scott, who increased public interest in the area in the 19th century through his poem *The Lady of the Lake,* and the novel *Rob Roy*, based on the outlaw Rob Roy MacGregor, who is buried at Balquhidder.

**ROUTE** From Stirling take the A84 north to Callander. As you enter the town look for a sign directing you to 'Golf Course and Bracklinn Falls'. Follow this road uphill, past Arden House – made famous in the TV drama *Doctor Finlay's Casebook* – to the Bracklinn Falls car park. A short walk of about 100 yards back downhill from the car park brings you to a path on your right, leading into the trees past the fenced-off public water supply. This path meets with a forestry road where again you turn right. Walk 50 yards along the road to where another path on your right breaks off and eventually leads to the summit. Continuing your circular walk, again turn right as you reach the summit taking the path east, past the Jubilee Cairn, until you reach the Braeleny road where your last right turn of the day takes you on a half mile tarmac walk back to the car.

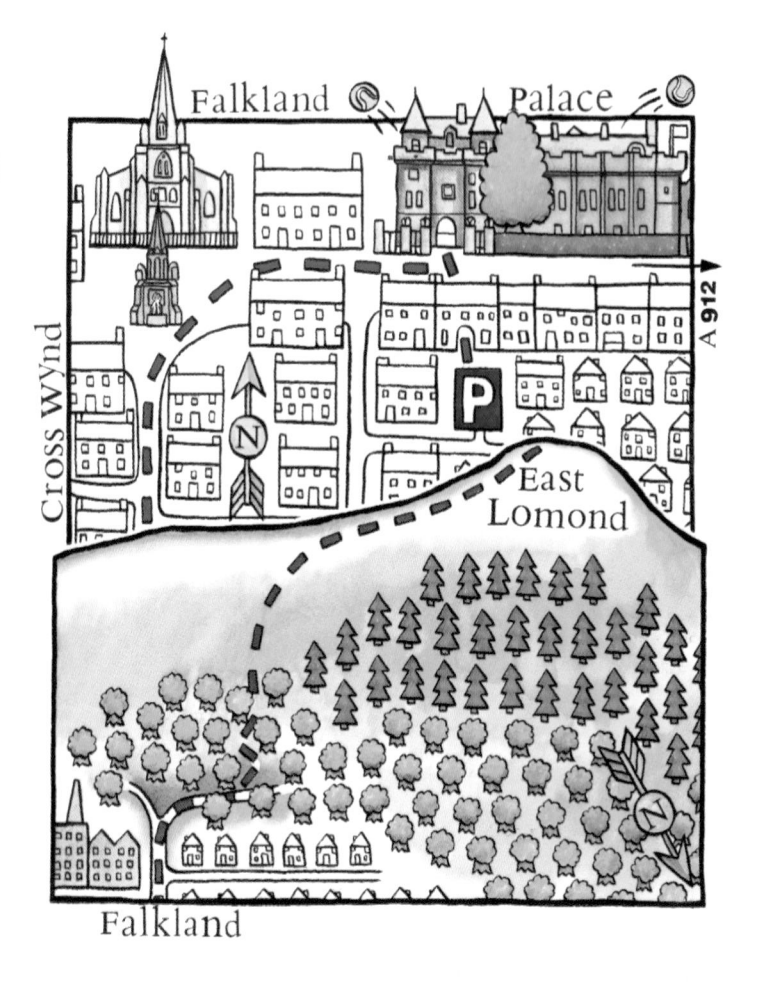

| MAP | OS Sheet 59, St Andrews, Kirkcaldy & Glenrothes |
|---|---|
| DISTANCE | 4 miles (6km) |
| RATING | Moderate. Good paths with a testing pull to the summit |
| GEAR | Walking boots and waterproofs |

# FALKLAND & EAST LOMOND

Adopted around 1460 as a royal residence by James II and transformed into a Renaissance house for James V, Falkland Palace is where the early Stewart Kings came to work, rest and play tennis.

**THEMES** Although tennis in its original French form was being played at Hampton Court prior to Falkland, the court at Falkland Palace in Fife lays claim to being the oldest in Britain. Built in 1539 for King James V, the court played host to a game bearing few similarities to the tennis played at Wimbledon today. A strange cross between lawn tennis, squash and chess with a racquet, the subtleties of 'Royal' or 'Real' tennis, by which name it is now known, make sure the winner is not always the person who serves the quickest or shouts the loudest. Surrounded by beautiful gardens, the court is still in regular use by the active Falkland Royal Tennis Court group. The village ranks with Fife's renowned East Neuk for attractiveness. The landscape of the county famously led King James VI of Scotland to describe the old kingdom of Fife as being like a beggar's mantle fringed with gold.

**ROUTE** Take the A92 trunk road from Kirkcaldy through Glenrothes, then the A912 to Falkland. Park in the large car park in the middle of town. Make your way to the Cross Wynd, which heads south from the Bruce Fountain towards the Lomond Hills. Pass the factory on your left – once a manufacturer of linoleum, which added a distinctive and rather unwelcome odour to the air. Now it's a food-packaging producer. Head up the waymarked path to a stairway with rustic wooden handrails by the side of the enclosed public water supply. Staying on this path you soon clear the trees where a prominent pathway leads south-west up steep slopes, through heather and over open moorland, to the peak of East Lomond, marked by a granite and bronze viewfinder. Return the same way.

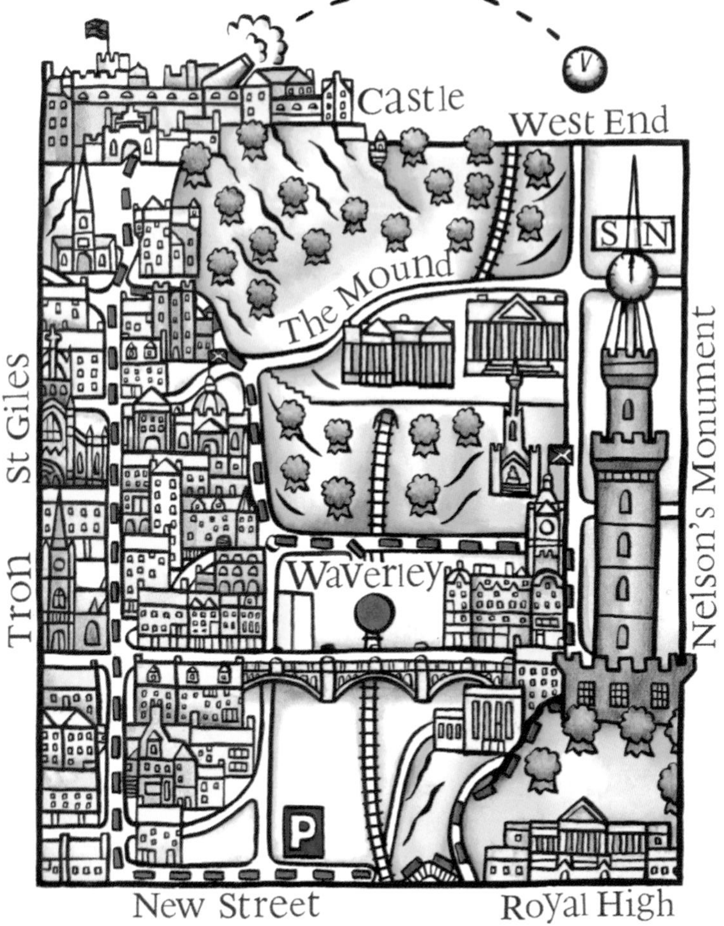

Castle

West End

The Mound

S N

St Giles

Nelson's Monument

Tron

Waverley

New Street

Royal High

| MAP | City Tour Guide |
|---|---|
| **DISTANCE** | 2.5 miles (4km) |
| **RATING** | Easy. Roads and pavements |
| **GEAR** | No special requirements |

# CASTLE TO CALTON HILL

In the historic streets of Scotland's capital, even the most popular tourist attractions have their quaint customs to reveal.

**THEMES** Nelson's Monument, which stands on Calton Hill, has been Edinburgh's alternative time signal since  1853. Consisting of a large white ball which on weekdays falls at the stroke of 12 noon, it was installed to enable the captains of ships moored on the Forth to set their chronometers accurately. In summer it coincides with the firing of the one-o-clock gun at the castle, and tourists are told the ball is used as target practice for the castle gunners! The walk takes in many historic sites of old Edinburgh, and there are panoramic views of the city from the hill, taking in the castle, Holyrood, Arthur's Seat, the  Firth of Forth, the New Town and Princes Street. As well as Nelson's Monument the hill also has its very own Acropolis, modelled on the Parthenon in Athens; but it was just an incomplete folly designed by architects C R Cockerell and the celebrated William Playfair.

**ROUTE** As parking in the capital can be difficult, travel to Waverley Station by train and make your way to the castle by The Mound and then the Lawnmarket. Leaving the castle, which houses Scotland's Crown Jewels and the Stone of Destiny, go back down to the High Street, popularly called the Royal Mile. Continuing down hill you pass St Giles Cathedral and Parliament Square on your right, the City Chambers on your left, and further down, the John Knox Museum. Turn off the High Street  into New Street. At the bottom you will find a small arched entry leading on to Jacob's Ladder. This stone stairway leads up to Regent's Road beside the Scottish Office building. Carefully cross Regent's Road and take the road round the back of the old Royal High School to Calton Hill. A stairway on the west side of the hill leads back down to Regent's Road, where a short walk west, along Waterloo Place, will take you to Princes Street and back to Waverley Station.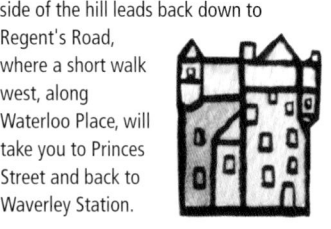

North Berwick Law

A 198

N

The Lodge

Auld Kirk

North Berwick

| MAP | OS Sheet 66, Edinburgh, Penicuik & North Berwick |
|---|---|
| DISTANCE | 3 miles (5km) |
| RATING | Easy. Roads, paths and open hill |
| GEAR | Strong footwear recommended |

# NORTH BERWICK LAW

On All Hallows Eve, October 31, 1590, when King James VI sailed back to Scotland with his 15-year-old bride, Princess Anne of Denmark, the reception committee wasn't quite what he had bargained for.

**THEMES** Flickering flames from black candles lit up the interior of the Old North Berwick Kirk, as a procession of over 200 warlocks and witches danced down the aisle in an unholy sabbath. The main purpose of the gathering was to destroy King James VI by means of sorcery as he sailed back from the continent with his young bride, the 15-year-old Princess Anne of Denmark. Although the treasure ship carrying the royal wedding gifts was sunk in the resulting maelstrom, the ship transporting the newlyweds was saved from destruction due to King James's 'great piety and saintliness'.

There has been a whale jawbone on the summit of North Berwick Law since 1709. The arch was renewed in the 1850s from an old Dunbar whaling ship and more recently replaced in 1936. There is no documentary evidence, however, to suggest that North Berwick was a whaling port. It's well worth visiting the seabird centre, which has some excellent displays and live video footage of the gannets on Bass Rock.

**ROUTE** North Berwick has long been a popular holiday resort, with views to Craigleith Island and the Bass Rock – best seen from the vantage point of North Berwick Law. From Edinburgh take the scenic coastal route, passing through Musselburgh, Prestonpans, Port Seton and Gullane before arriving at the seaside resort. Starting your walk from the Auld Kirk, where Agnes Sampson and her coven of witches gathered in 1590, walk south towards the tourist information centre and pass through a gate and arch into the grounds of The Lodge, from where 'The Law' looms ahead. Continue south and follow the signs into Couper Avenue and Wishart Avenue before reaching Berwick Law's designated car park, just off the B1347. From the car park, cross over a stile and turn right on a clear pathway to the top. Berwick Law is a scheduled monument with signs of an Iron Age hill fort on the summit, along with a Napoleonic watchtower and the whale jawbone.

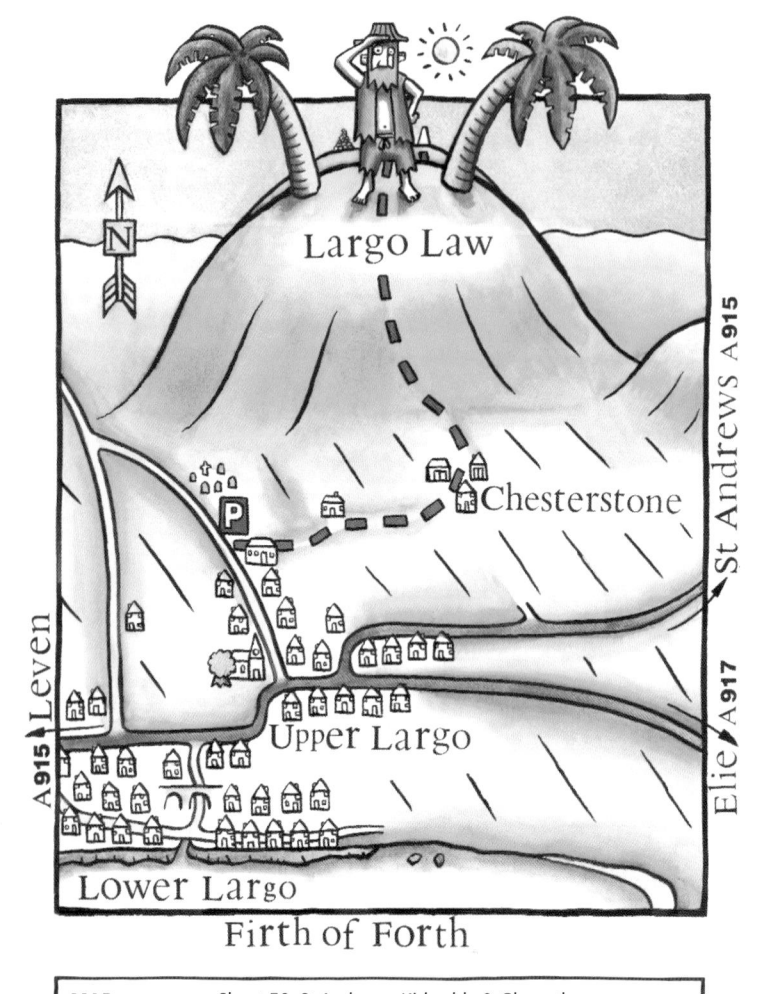

| MAP | Sheet 59, St Andrews, Kirkcaldy & Glenrothes |
|-----|---------------------------------------------|
| DISTANCE | 2.5 miles (4km) |
| RATING | Easy. An easy scramble up grassy slopes |
| GEAR | Stout footwear and windproof clothing |

Arthur's Seat

Salisbury Crags

Meadowbank

Railway, now tarmaced over as a cycleway, was one of Scotland's earliest lines, running between Dalkeith and Edinburgh. Horses at first provided the power to haul freight, then the line became hugely popular as a passenger route. For youngsters doing this walk there is the novelty of going through a well-lit tunnel on the return leg.

**ROUTE** Start from car park next to St Margaret's Loch or behind Holyrood House. From either car park take the grassy paths below the ruins of St Anthony's Chapel and head for Arthur's Seat. There are several ways to approach the peak. I like to take the prominent little ridge called Long Row. Climb steadily along this with views constantly opening up on all sides. At the end of Long Row an obvious path curves around to the left, then back right up to the summit of Arthur's Seat. Take care not to slip on the well-worn summit rocks. The view stretches for miles in all directions. From the top, a wide, grassy path angling south and slightly east can be seen. Descend to this and follow it round to the left, directionally due east along a narrower path between gorse bushes, with Duddingston Loch prominent below. The path emerges on to the road circling Arthur's Seat at a sharp bend. Cross the road, go down a few steps, then a path, and finally right down a long line of steps to reach Duddingston Loch on the edge of Duddingston Village. Go left into the village and perhaps enjoy some refreshment at the Sheep Heid Inn before continuing east along the main road to a junction. Turn right and follow the road round to where a blue cycle route sign is encountered, just past the entrance to Duddingston golf course. Cross the road and take the Innocent Railway back towards the city centre. Walk through a tunnel which emerges in the courtyard of a block of flats. Go through the courtyard for a short way and up some steps on the left. Turn left past the flats, then left again to emerge eventually on Queen's Drive under Salisbury Crags. Either take the path high up under the crags or, more easily, along the wide, grassy verge by the roadside to the start point.

Salisbury Crags

Arthur's Seat

Pollock Halls

Holyrood

Duddingston

Meadowbank

| MAP | OS Pathfinder 407, Edinburgh |
|---|---|
| DISTANCE | 4.5 miles (7km) |
| RATING | Easy. Hill paths and pavement |
| GEAR | Boots recommended |

# 44

# BUACHAILLE ETIVE BEAG

Living in the shadow of a big brother can be a bit daunting, but the Wee Buachaille has two Munros to offer and provides an excellent outing by any standards.

**THEMES** The A82 road that crosses Rannoch Moor and drops down into Glencoe is a route full of mountain drama. Guarding the portal to the glen is Buachaille Etive Mor, the great herdsman of Etive, whose formidable crags have been the haunt of climbers for decades. Next door is the little herdsman, brother to the Three Sisters of Beinn Fhada, Gearr Aonach and Aonach Dubh – a feminine trio no Young Turk should trifle with lightly. No Scot needs reminding of the famous massacre in the glen, of course. Thankfully clans Campbell and Macdonald live more amicably these days, and any battling is reserved for mountaineers getting to grips with the challenges of buttresses, rock walls and ridges. In the depths of winter the scenery here can be stunningly beautiful, but even more than in summer needs to be treated with sound judgment and respect. For those who possess the necessary skills, however, there is no finer place to be in the whole of Scotland on a clear day, with the snow and ice glistening in the sunlight

and a blue sky above. Since Glencoe is owned by the National Trust for Scotland there is access all year round, with no restrictions at this time of year for stalking.

**ROUTE** On the left hand side going down Glencoe, where its jaws narrow is The Study, notable for the impressive volume of water tumbling into the River Coe. Back up the glen a short way is a cairn marking the beginning of the Lairig Eilde pass to Glen Etive. Buachaille Etive Beag towers up on the left. Take the path, heading for the point where it crosses the Allt Lairig Eilde. Shortly before this, a fairly indistinct path cuts off left up the slopes of Stob Coire Raineach. Take this, climbing steadily to an obvious dip in the ridge above. Once at this bealach, turn left to gain the summit of Stob Coire Raineach. Return to the bealach and follow the ridge along, with glorious views, to the higher Munro summit of Stob Dubh, looking straight into Glen Etive.

A rest and refreshments stop will leave you ready to tackle the descent into the Lairig Eilde. Carefully make your way north west off Stob Dubh to pick up the path running through the pass, and thence back to your start point.

Three Sisters

Buachaille Etive Mor

Buachaille Etive Beag

Pass of Glencoe

A82

| MAP | OS 41 Ben Nevis |
|---|---|
| DISTANCE | 5 miles (8km) |
| RATING | Strenuous. Rough hill paths, scree grass and boulders |
| GEAR | Full hill-walking kit |

# 45

# DUMGOYNE

Is it a hill or is it a mountain? At 1,402ft, the sense of giddiness experienced on the summit may be more to do with the distillery in the glen below than the rarefied atmosphere.

**THEMES** Ten years after the act of 1823 made it viable to distil whisky legally, due to a reduction in duty, the Glengoyne distillery was established. Making good use of the Glengoyne Burn running down from the hill above, this centre of whisky production is said to give back to the surrounding hillside 2% of its product in evaporation each year. Known as the Angels' Share, this is equivalent to 100,000 bottles. As you reach the summit there is a magic in the air that makes you want to sing a few bars of 'I Belong to Glasgow'. But be careful, a heavenly chorus of giddy angels, wafting its way up from the glen, may accompany you.

**ROUTE** Dumgoyne is 15 miles north of Glasgow, to the rear of the Glengoyne distillery, on the A81 Aberfoyle road, near the village of Killearn. Park your car beside the bonded warehouses, cross the main road and go left about 100yds. Take the private road up past the houses. This road, winding through delightful mixed forestry, soon joins the old drove road heading over to Killearn from Blanefield. Where the roads meet, go through a metal gate and cross the open pasture, planted with hawthorn trees. After crossing a burn at the far end of the field, an obvious track leads to the summit through the crags and rocky outcrops that are a distinctive feature of the area. A hill with more attitude than altitude, Dumgoyne was a volcanic vent plug, with traces of the hard lava forming its core still evident on the summit.

Dumgoyne

Killearn ▲ Loch Lomond

A81 ▼ Glasgow

P

Glengoyne Distillery

| MAP | OS Sheet 57, Stirling & Trossachs area |
|---|---|
| DISTANCE | 3 miles (5km) |
| RATING | Easy. A short, steep climb up grassy slopes |
| GEAR | Boots with good grips are a sensible option |

# 46

# DUNS LAW & HEN POO

Stand in the corner with your dunce's hat on in preparation for this jaunt with connections to the cerebral environment of Oxford and Duns Scotus.

**THEMES** Arguably the most important scholar to leave Scotland in any millennium was Johannes Duns Scotus. Known as the Angelic Doctor and nicknamed Doctor Subtilis because of his theological arguments, he is said to have attracted 30,000 students to his lectures while teaching at Oxford. Born a native of Duns in 1265, his teachings on philosophy and theology were much sought after, and he was invited to lecture in Paris and Cologne. Originator of the realist view of practical faith, opposing the theoretical view established by Aristotle, Duns Scotus gave a new word to the English language: 'dunce', from the derisive Duns' Man, which was given to followers of his teachings.

**ROUTE** Unravelling the complexities of the Borders road network can be scenically rewarding, but challenging. So unless you are accompanied by a proficient co-pilot, the best route to Duns from Scotland's central belt would be to take the A1 to Grantshouse, south of Dunbar, then the A6112 into the town. Starting your walk from the market square go north, crossing the main road junction, and continue till you come to the lodge house of Duns Castle Estate. Entering the estate here, take the first path on your right through mixed woodland to climb Duns Law. It was here, in 1639, that David Leslie's Covenanting forces came for a tête-à-tête with the Royalist army of King Charles I. Views from the flat summit take in most of East Berwickshire. There is a memorial to the soldiers of the Covenant. Retracing your steps back to the access road, the next path on your right takes you on an anti-clockwise circuit of the loch known as the Hen Poo. The track round the loch, which has lots of water fowl, eventually brings you back to your starting point after passing a stone paying homage to Duns Scotus.

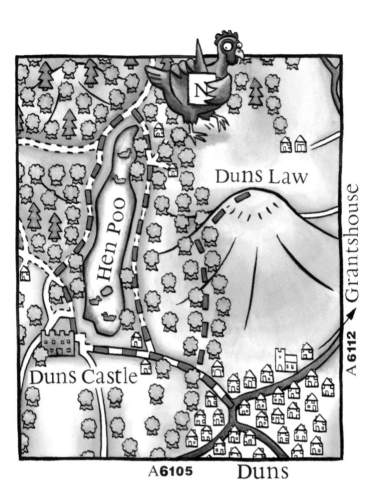

Duns Law

Hen Poo

Duns Castle

Duns

A**6105**

A **6112** ← Grantshouse

| MAP | OS Sheet 74, Kelso & Coldstream, Jedburgh & Duns |
|---|---|
| DISTANCE | 4 miles (6km) |
| RATING | Easy. Good paths, tracks and road |
| GEAR | Boots and a waterproof |

# 47

# BEINN RESIPOL

The Ardnamurchan peninsula is as far west as you can get on mainland Britain, and the feeling of remote wilderness is inescapable.

**THEMES** Often swept by rainclouds brought in on westerly winds over the sea, Ardnamurchan is nevertheless an incredibly beautiful place — even more so when the sun does shine. The quickest way to get there, avoiding a long drive round by Fort William, is to cross on the Corran ferry from Onich. The sense of wilderness increases by the mile as you drive along the A861 towards Strontian. Red deer, seals, otters and the lord of the skies, the golden eagle, rule this landscape. All of them and more can be seen with patience and a little luck. Ruined crofts are reminders of the harsh rural lifestyle of earlier years, while the remains of Iron Age forts, standing stones and chambered cairns are evidence of even earlier human occupation. For walkers the going can be tough, with fewer defined paths on hill ground than elsewhere, but extremely rewarding. Shorter, more amenable routes are also on offer. Forest Enterprise has developed a series of lovely shore and woodland walks that are a delight. Try Ariundle oakwood for example — a circular meander along the banks of the River Strontian and through some ancient oaks. It's an excellent introduction to the area.

**ROUTE** From Strontian take the minor road signed to Polloch. On reaching the hamlet of Ariundle — no more than a few houses — turn sharp left and park off to the side of the track near a gate, being careful not to cause an obstruction. Head along the track past the gate and continue to an isolated tree, turning right to follow the old miners' track north west. The chemical element strontium was discovered here and mined, acquiring its name from the village of Strontian. Climb steadily along the track to a high point marked by some large cairns. The east ridge of Beinn Resipol is now clearly visible to the left, rising to the summit. Continue with the track for a short way before cutting left across rough and often boggy ground to gain the east ridge. The lack of an identifiable path makes the going slow, but the stretch is mercifully short. Once on the ridge things improve markedly. Head along the ridge and over a false summit, cross a grassy area and make the final ascent to a large cairn on top. If it's clear, the reward is an unobstructed view out over the sea, with the islands of Rum, Eigg and Muck sticking out of the ocean like giant whales. Return the same way.

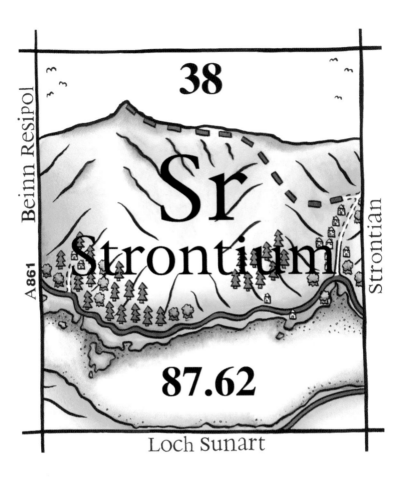

| MAP | OS 40 Loch Shiel |
| --- | --- |
| DISTANCE | 8 miles there and back (13km) |
| RATING | Strenuous. Track, mountain paths and a boggy section |
| GEAR | Full hill-walking kit |

# 48

# BRAEMAR CIRCUIT

The Deeside village of Braemar is inextricably linked with royalty. Apart from the Highland seat of Balmoral there is Crathie Church on the approach to the village, where members of the Royal Family worship when they are in the area.

**THEMES** Braemar often ranks as one of the coldest places in Britain in winter, but the scenery here surely vies with some of grandest and most splendid in Britain. Under snow it is magical, and for Prince Charles at least, the craggy eminence of Lochnagar and the loch beneath it are special, inspiring his children's tale about The Old Man of Lochnagar. In recent years the village centre has undergone something of a transformation, increasing its attraction as a tourist destination with something to offer all year round. The Royal Highland Gathering that takes place on the first Saturday in September dates back around 900 years to the time when Malcolm Canmore summoned the clans to pit their strength against one another, enabling him to choose the best as his soldiers. Part of our route follows the old carriage road enjoyed by Queen Victoria, who often stopped, it is said, to give money to children she encountered on the way. Speculation has always surrounded the queen's relationship with her ghillie, John Brown, which gave rise to the film *Mrs Brown*, starring Judi Dench and Billy Connolly.

**ROUTE** The walk takes a circuit below Creag Choinnich, the small hill to the east of Braemar. It starts near St Margaret's Church. A stile behind the church gives access to a woodland track. Follow the track until it narrows to a footpath. Carry on steadily upwards until the path emerges from the trees and joins another track. Turn left along this and follow it on a slight upward gradient to a prominent cliff, known locally as the Lion's Face Crag. Close up it is difficult to see any resemblance to a lion. Those with imagination looking from Invercauld, below, might discern something – a bit like Edinburgh's Arthur's Seat has the look of a sleeping lion from certain angles. The view from the crag to Invercauld is worth the climb. Return to the earlier junction and take the wide track known as the Queen's Drive down to a gate on the A93. Go through the gate and turn right along the road back into Braemar, passing the house where Robert Louis Stevenson stayed when he was writing *Treasure Island* in 1881. Follow the road back to the start.

| **MAP** | OS 43, Braemar |
| --- | --- |
| **DISTANCE** | 3 miles (5km) |
| **RATING** | Easy. Good paths |
| **GEAR** | Boots advisable, in the wet especially. |

# ISLE OF KERRERA

This small island on the west coast, opposite the busy tourist Mecca of Oban, offers a pleasant refuge from the mainland summer bustle and a walk following in the footsteps of cattle drovers.

**THEMES** If fairytale castles are your thing, then look no further than this hilly little island, only five miles long. Gylen Castle, Renaissance stronghold of the MacDougall clan, by whom it was built, sits on a rocky headland at the south end of the island overlooking Castle Bay. Its walls still stand intact, rising to full height with some interesting carved relief on the north wall. The castle was sacked during the 17th-century Scottish wars of the Covenant. Carn Breugach, a high point with a trig pillar on top, provides fine views of the surrounding islands and the mainland peaks, though bracken can make the half hour or so ascent from the ferry jetty quite trying in summer. Kerrera was once a staging post for cattle being brought across from the much larger neighbouring island of Mull to marts on the mainland. The famous brooch of Lorn, stolen by the MacDougalls from the fugitive King Robert the Bruce, was later taken from Gylen by the Campbells, but returned to the MacDougalls in modern times.

**ROUTE** As with all crossings to islands, there is an excitement about the short ride over the Sound of Kerrera from the mainland, in anticipation of what's to come. The ferry leaves from a jetty on the coast road around two miles south of Oban. There is a regular service which also runs on demand (tel: 01631 563665). On landing follow the track south past Horseshoe Bay and Little Horseshoe Bay, both deriving their names from their obvious shape. Pass Upper Gylen farm, heading for Lower Gylen. Access to the castle is through a gate just before Lower Gylen. Rejoin the main track again which traverses above Castle Bay, then turns north past a deserted house. Approaching Barnabuck farm, the path divides. Take the lower fork and head across high ground turning gradually east, back towards the jetty, descending past Balliemore and the old church, now a school.

| | |
|---|---|
| **MAP** | OS 49 Oban and East Mull |
| **DISTANCE** | 7 miles (11km) |
| **RATING** | Moderate. Tracks and paths |
| **GEAR** | Hill-walking gear with provisions for the day's outing |

# 50

# LOCH ETIVE SHORE

With Glen Etive in cloud, thoughts of mountain summits are all you have. Blessed with a clear day the tops are stunning – but views from on high are not always the best, as this route proves all too well.

**THEMES** Be thankful when the cloudbase is down about the 1,000ft level when you drive down the twisting Glen Etive road to the start of this walk. On a clear day there is a severe risk of sustaining whiplash injury as you crane your neck looking up at the masses of grey granite on either side, or worse still, running the car off the road as you become hypnotised, eyeing the glen scenery. Most people are put off by this winding road leading to the head of Loch Etive, but persevere and you will find there are few other glens that offer the same feeling of remoteness or solitude within a relatively short, 13-mile drive of a main trunk road – the A82 to Glen Coe. Ben Starav, a fine Munro at 3,541ft, guards the east side of Loch Etive. Above the lochside path on the west side is Ben Trilleachan. Its steep granite slabs attract the attentions of agile rock climbers, who need delicate footwork and a very bold approach to succeed. The view looking back towards Glen Coe is a classic, and has featured on many a postcard and calendar.

In summer, boat tours run from Taynuilt up the loch to view the scenery and get a close-up of the seals which sun themselves out of the water.

**ROUTE** Driving north over the Rannoch Moor towards Glen Coe, turn off the A82 opposite the King's House road end, signposted for Glen Etive, and twist down to park at the head of Loch Etive beside a ruined pier. Loch Etive – a sea loch stretching 18 miles inland from the tidal Falls of Lora at Connel Bridge – has often been compared to the fjords of Norway due to the rocky hills and mixed woodland of birch, oak, hazel and holly: remnants of the great Caledonian forest that once covered most of the country. Following the path, running along the west bank of the loch for about three miles, will give you an idea of what this area has to offer, with a good chance of seeing cormorants in the water, deer in the woodland and golden eagles over the hills. If it's human company you're looking for, you had better take it with you.

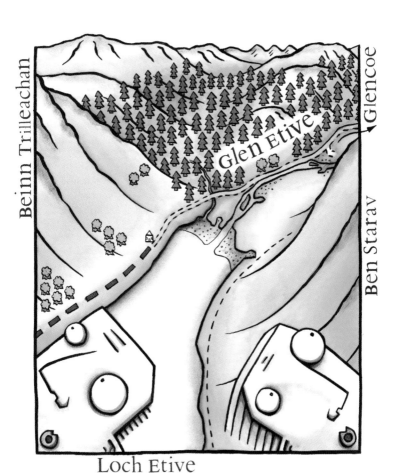

| MAP | OS Sheet 50, Glen Orchy |
| --- | --- |
| DISTANCE | 6 miles (10km) |
| RATING | Moderate. Rough, gluey footpath in an isolated area |
| GEAR | Boots and gaiters, or wellies. |

# 51

# FIFE COASTAL PATH, ELIE TO SHELL BAY

The view from the East Neuk of Fife across the Forth is often obscured by early morning haar. But when the mists roll away, the seascape opens up.

**THEMES** On November 21, 1918, the banks of the Fife coast were crowded as people flocked to witness the submission of Germany's fleet. Flanked by 60 allied battleships, with another 120 light cruisers and destroyers, the German flotilla of 70 ships steamed towards Rosyth to surrender their flag to Admiral Sir David Beatty, Commander in Chief of the Allied Naval Forces. After two days anchored in the Firth of Forth, the German Navy set sail under heavy escort to Orkney, where, seven months later, on June 21, 1919, they scuttled their entire fleet at Scapa Flow.

**ROUTE** From Kirkcaldy take the A915, then the A917, to Elie, parking at the East Links car park and picnic area. From the car park pick up the Fife Coast Path at the Lady's Tower, a summer gazebo built in the late 18th century for Janet Fall (Lady Anstruther) of Elie House. From Lady's Tower, follow the coastline west passing the lighthouse at Elie Ness, the harbour and sands of Elie Bay, and on to the adjoining village of Earlsferry. Continuing on the waymarked coastal path through the golf course, head for the path that takes you above the cliffs to Kincraig Point, where you come upon an old concrete gun emplacement – a relic left from the Second World War. From here follow the coast path round to the sand dunes and beach of Shell Bay. Now decide whether you wish to return the way you came or walk on to Lower Largo, where public transport will take you back to Elie. (Check timetable with local bus company.)

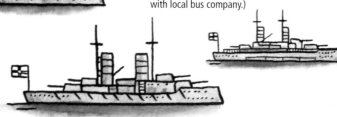

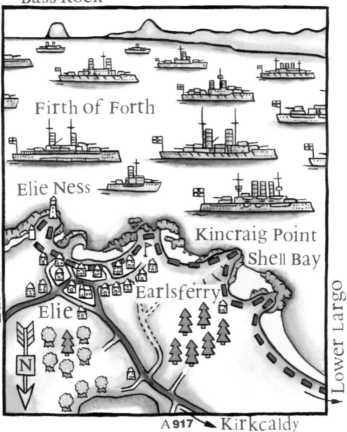

| | |
|---|---|
| **MAP** | OS Sheet 59, St Andrews, Kirkcaldy & Glenrothes |
| **DISTANCE** | 8 miles (13km) |
| **RATING** | Moderate. Exposed coastal walk above cliffs |
| **GEAR** | Stout footwear and seasonable clothing. |

# DUN DA LAMH, KINGUSSIE

Imagine yourself as a Pictish chieftain, scanning the Speyside landscape from your fortress set high on a hill, to keep your tribe safe from harm.

**THEMES** There are some woodland walks I wouldn't give a thank-you for, following monotonous forestry access roads through pines with no real scenic value. On the other hand, the forestry companies have come to realise the need to make woodlands not only accessible but interesting. Provision for walkers, mountain bikers and horse riders is increasingly seen as a necessary part of woodland planning and management, and amongst the host of walks of varying lengths available there are some real gems. This one offers an excellent half-day circuit with stunning views and archaeological remains to create further attraction. It's on Forestry Commission property in Strathmashie, off the A86 Spean Bridge to Newtonmore road near Laggan village. There are good car parking bays on both sides of the road and the route is waymarked, making it easy to follow. The archaeological interest is provided by the remains of an ancient hill fort called Dun da Lamh – the fort of two hands. Probably first constructed in the later Bronze Age, about 3,000 years ago, it is likely to have been reoccupied by a Pictish chieftain. Situated on a high knoll – Black Craig – it was clearly a great defensive vantage point providing views over the surrounding countryside.

**ROUTE** From the car park on the south side of the road, follow blue waymarkers to link with a broad forest road that climbs up through mature pines. There's not much to grab the attention until you emerge from the trees and the scenery begins to open up. Look for a waymarker that takes you sharp left off the forest road on a narrower path fairly steeply uphill to a summit. There's a magnificent view from here, especially of the Ardverikie hills and Creag Meagaidh. Continue along the path which drops quite sharply downhill after a while, using wooden steps, to a clearing. There's a plinth marking the base of the short uphill path to Dun da Lamh, a scheduled ancient monument with a rampart that was 18ft thick in places – typical of the defences that surrounded Pictish royal sites. It may well have been the frontier fortress of a great Pictish nation that occupied these lands in round houses, grouped into farmsteads. Head back down to the plinth, then take the track leading downhill back towards the start. At a forest road junction look ahead for a new section of made path through felled trees that emerges on a forest road. You can either follow this to the start or, more easily, walk alongside the A86 for a short distance to end up at the same point.

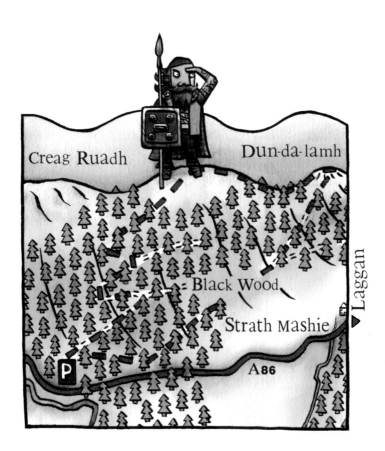

Creag Ruadh

Dun-da-lamh

Black Wood

Strath Mashie

Laggan

A86

P

| MAP | OS 35 Kingussie |
| --- | --- |
| DISTANCE | 5 miles (8km) |
| RATING | Moderate. Forest road and paths |
| GEAR | Boots and a waterproof |

# BIOGRAPHIES

## PETER EVANS

Peter Evans moved to Scotland from his native South Wales more than 20 years ago. He is a former editor of *The Great Outdoors* magazine for walkers and *Climber* magazine, and has walked and climbed across Scotland in all seasons. Presently a production journalist with *Scotland on Sunday* and a writer of its Walk of the Week, he is also a passionate advocate for the environment and has written many articles on subjects in that field of journalism. Together with his wife and two daughters, Peter lives in the Clackmannanshire town of Dollar, under the Ochils.

## JAMES MCDONALD

Born Laurieston by Falkirk, June 1952. By necessity, a full time painter and decorator through the week, but come the weekend he combines his hobbies of walking and writing by "Lifting my eyes to the hills and straddling the summits with my soul." Chairman of Falkirk Writers' Circle 2004-2005.

## GLEN MCBETH

Glen McBeth has been working as a freelance illustrator for over ten years. His distinctive and highly original work has appeared in magazines and newspapers around the world and has featured in various design and advertising projects. Glen's map illustrations began with the Walk of the Week feature in *Scotland on Sunday* and have been a part of the feature for several years. His maps aim to show a representation of the terrain and the colourful folklore and stories associated with the walk.

www.glenmcbeth.co.uk

# WALKS
# RATING
# INDEX

| EASY | WALK | | WALK |
|------|------|---|------|
| THE DEIL'S CAULDRON | 1 | FETLAR | 19 |
| BALLATER BRIDGES | 2 | MEIKLE BIN | 22 |
| ROSLIN GLEN | 6 | THE EILDON HILLS | 25 |
| MONUMENT HILL, DALMALLY | 9 | FALLS OF CLYDE | 26 |
| THE KNOCK OF CRIEFF | 10 | TINTO HILL | 28 |
| ST ANDREWS | 13 | BIRNAM HILL | 31 |
| THE WHANGIE | 15 | FALKLAND & EAST LOMOND | 38 |
| ANSTRUTHER TO CRAIL | 17 | CALLANDER CRAGS | 39 |
| STACKS OF DUNCANSBY | 21 | THE PAP OF GLENCOE | 41 |
| CALLENDAR PARK | 24 | WEST LOMOND | 42 |
| LINLITHGOW TO COCKLEROY | 27 | ISLE OF KERRERA | 49 |
| LOCH AN EILEIN | 33 | LOCH ETIVE SHORE | 50 |
| LOCH TROOL | 34 | ELIE TO SHELL BAY | 51 |
| LARGO LAW | 35 | | |
| NORTH BERWICK LAW | 36 | | |
| CASTLE TO CALTON HILL | 37 | HARD | |
| THE BURNS TRAIL | 40 | GLEN FINGLAS | 4 |
| ARTHUR'S SEAT | 43 | BEN LOMOND | 5 |
| DUMGOYNE | 45 | MOUNT KEEN | 7 |
| DUNS LAW & HEN POO | 46 | THE COBBLER | 11 |
| BRAEMAR CIRCUIT | 48 | RAILWAY RAMBLE, KILLIN | 14 |
| DUN DA LAMH | 52 | BEN VENUE | 16 |
| | | BEN VRACKIE | 20 |
| | | BEN NEVIS | 23 |
| MODERATE | | SCHIEHALLION | 29 |
| ST ABB'S HEAD | 3 | BEINN EIGHE | 30 |
| THE OCHILS | 8 | DUN CAAN | 32 |
| THE GREENOCK CUT | 12 | BUACHAILLE ETIVE BEAG | 44 |
| BEN A'AN | 18 | BEINN RESIPOL | 47 |

# ALPHABETICAL INDEX

| A | WALK | G | WALK |
|---|---|---|---|
| ANSTRUTHER TO CRAIL | 17 | GLEN FINGLAS | 4 |
| ARTHUR'S SEAT | 43 | GREENOCK CUT, THE | 12 |
| **B** | | **K** | |
| BALLATER BRIDGES | 2 | KERRERA, ISLE OF | 49 |
| BEINN EIGHE | 30 | KNOCK OF CRIEFF, THE | 10 |
| BEINN RESIPOL | 47 | **L** | |
| BEN A'AN | 18 | LARGO LAW | 35 |
| BEN LOMOND | 5 | LINLITHGOW TO COCKLEROY | 27 |
| BEN NEVIS | 23 | LOCH AN EILEIN | 33 |
| BEN VENUE | 16 | LOCH TROOL | 34 |
| BEN VRACKIE | 20 | **M** | |
| BIRNAM HILL | 31 | MEIKLE BIN | 22 |
| BRAEMAR CIRCUIT | 48 | MONUMENT HILL, DALMALLY | 9 |
| BUACHAILLE ETIVE BEAG | 44 | MOUNT KEEN | 7 |
| BURNS TRAIL | 40 | **N** | |
| **C** | | NORTH BERWICK LAW | 36 |
| CALLANDER CRAGS | 39 | **O** | |
| CALLENDAR PARK | 24 | OCHILS, THE | 8 |
| CASTLE TO CALTON HILL | 37 | **P** | |
| COBBLER, THE | 11 | PAP OF GLENCOE, THE | 41 |
| **D** | | **R** | |
| DEIL'S CAULDRON, THE | 1 | RAILWAY RAMBLE, KILLIN | 14 |
| DUMGOYNE | 45 | ROSLIN GLEN | 6 |
| DUN CAAN | 32 | **S** | |
| DUN DA LAMH | 52 | ST ABB'S HEAD | 3 |
| DUNS LAW & HEN POO | 46 | ST ANDREWS | 13 |
| **E** | | SCHIEHALLION | 29 |
| EILDON HILLS, THE | 25 | STACKS OF DUNCANSBY | 21 |
| ELIE TO SHELL BAY | 51 | **T** | |
| ETIVE SHORE | 50 | TINTO HILL | 28 |
| **F** | | **W** | |
| FALKLAND & EAST LOMOND | 38 | WEST LOMOND | 42 |
| FALLS OF CLYDE | 26 | WHANGIE, THE | 15 |
| FETLAR | 19 | | |